Hospice
A Memoir of Life among the Dying

Deborah Lee

BookLocker
Saint Petersburg, Florida

Print ISBN: 978-1-64718-973-0
Epub ISBN: 978-1-64718-974-7
Mobi ISBN: 978-1-64718-975-4

Published by BookLocker.com, Inc., St. Petersburg, Florida.

Printed on acid-free paper.

BookLocker.com, Inc.
2020

First Edition

Library of Congress Cataloging in Publication Data
Lee, Deborah
Hospice: A Memoir of Life among the Dying by Deborah Lee
Library of Congress Control Number: 2020917582

Contents

Introduction: Why I Do This Work

I wish I had a nickel for every person who has said to me, over the years, "I don't know *how* you do this" (meaning, hospice work). That is almost always followed by one of two sentences: either the question (voiced rhetorically), "Don't you find it *depressing?*", or the pronouncement, "You must be a *really special* person." Perhaps we hospice workers are indeed special people – I can't say. But I *can* say with some authority that we are *not* all depressed about it, and that the motivations for – and gratifications from – the work we do are varied and might surprise you.

Just for the record, I did not grow up knowing that I wanted to work with dying people. As far back as I can remember, however, I had a degree of fascination with medical things. As a toddler, I used to stick band-aids all over my dolls and stuffed animals, and nurse them back to health. But though I contemplated nursing as one career possibility, I also at other times considered teacher, legal secretary, chef, fashion model, and singer in a rock band, just to name a few.

When I was fourteen years old, my paternal grandmother died. We were not close: my parents had divorced many years earlier, and there was no love lost between my mother and her former mother-in-law, so my limited contact with Grandma Milly was colored by the lingering animosity between my parents, and between my grandparents and their former children-in-law. All I understood was that Grandma had been stricken with bizarre and terrifying symptoms while traveling abroad with Grandpa, she had been air-ambulanced home, and diagnosed with a cancerous brain tumor. All of this was so utterly foreign to my experiences in life up to that point that I could not even formulate meaningful questions to ask. I remember being told that her disease was incurable and that she was expected to die from it, but I had no idea what that process would be like. At some point – and I don't recall whether I *asked* to visit her or whether someone decided I *ought* to visit her – my mother took me to the hospital. In retrospect, it could not have been easy for her to take me to see her former mother-in-law. I had been told that Grandma could not speak, but nothing prepared me for the sight of her in the hospital bed. Although she was always on the short side, she had also (at least during my lifetime) always been a heavy-set woman, typical of her Russian Jewish ancestors; she also had a strong personality, and that, combined with her stoutness, had given her a larger-than-life presence. Now she had wasted away to perhaps 75 pounds, and barely made a lump under the bedclothes. In the disinfectant-scented hospital room, she was connected to tubes and gizmos which I could not comprehend. Indeed she could not talk, and possibly she could not see either. My memory goes blank at this point. I don't remember if I hugged, or even touched, her. I don't remember what, if anything, my mother or I said to her. I remember only one thing from that moment: I was terrified! I asked no questions, because I was incapable of formulating a coherent thought. The whole experience became, in an instant, a door that I did not dare open, because what lay behind it was unspeakable. I never saw my grandmother again, and I did not open that door in my mind for many, many years. Writing about it even now, my eyes fill with tears….

The year that I started college, I discovered Elisabeth Kübler-Ross' magnum opus, *On Death and Dying*, and was spellbound by it. As a teenager, I was beginning to chart a course in life as one who rushed in where angels fear to tread, and traditionally-taboo subjects such as sex and religion were some of my favorite topics. I was repelled by superficiality, and wanted in all my social dealings to get beneath the surface to things that were *real*. Kübler-Ross added death and dying to my conversational repertoire. I was astonished to learn that there was at least one person on earth who had *fashioned a career* out of talking about things that one is not supposed to talk about. I began to consider seriously how I could follow in her mighty footsteps.

Someone once quipped that "life is what happens while you're busy making other plans." In my case, life indeed intervened, coupled with my boundless determination to cram in every possible experience – the wackier, the better – that life had to offer. At this point, let us hit fast-forward: I was now 32 years old, married, with a master's degree in social work, and one year of post-graduate employment in a family service agency under my belt. I was sitting at home on maternity leave, contemplating my rather ungratifying job situation, and debating whether to return to it. I picked up a social work publication and there, before my eyes, was a display ad for a hospice that was hiring social workers. I immediately concluded that this was some sort of sign from God. I stuffed my chubby, post-baby body into my only nice suit and (with the waistband precariously pinned because it wouldn't button) went on an interview. It was June of 1989. For some crazy reason, I was hired on the spot. The rest, as they say, is history....

You might think, since we work day in and day out with dying people, that we simply become immune to it, or worse yet, that we are hardened to the point that the pain and suffering all around us no longer affects us. Perish the thought! But I will let you in on one of the reasons we are able to do what we do: we don't see the ghosts that you see. I don't mean ghosts as in a scary movie. I mean ghosts as in the shadows of all the roles that your loved one used to play before he or she became terminally ill. When you look at Grandpa, you don't see him just as he is right this minute – you see how thin and frail he looks compared to the strong man who used to play football with you in the yard, how confused he is now compared to the brilliant attorney he once was, and how depressed he seems compared to the jolly soul who used to make everyone else laugh. We don't know all those other Grandpas. We see an emaciated, anxious, sad, disoriented, distressed individual, and we know that we can make those problems at least somewhat better. We know that we can – in most cases – grant him some quality of life to spend with his loved ones before he dies. We are moved by Grandpa's suffering, and that of the people who care about him. But we go home at the end of most days feeling that we have made some improvement in his situation.

I have just retired, after thirty years in the world of hospice. I gradually realized, as I delved into this career, that I was having some unique experiences that others might find interesting. There are a number of excellent memoirs written by hospice nurses, but I have not seen any written by hospice social workers. I first began setting pen to paper (or fingers to keyboard) about twenty years ago. The goals of this book are two-fold: to educate new workers and hospice families about what hospice really is and does, and to pull back the curtain for the general public on a strange and fascinating world that is rarely seen except by those who work in this field. To that end, I have gathered up the stories of many patients and families that I have encountered in the course of my lengthy hospice career. All names of patients and their families have been changed for confidentiality reasons (as well as the names of most coworkers mentioned herein), and I have also altered minor personal details to further obscure patient identities.

1

There's a Lot They Don't Teach You in Graduate School

Graciela Hernandez was fifteen years old and dying of a brain tumor. I had only been a hospice social worker for about a year and a half when my team manager Larry asked me to go see her family right away. The issue, my manager told me, was that the parents were very dissatisfied with our nurse Peggy, and Larry had not been able to get a good understanding of what the problem was. I was filled with dread at the thought of making this visit. First of all, pediatric hospice is something that I personally have a really hard time with. A 90-year-old dying of end-stage dementia is not necessarily a tragedy. Even a 50-year-old dying of cancer, although the situation may be terribly sad, is somewhat understandable – he or she has at least had some time to live life. But a *child* dying is a sucker punch to the gut – tragic, wrong, unfair, unthinkable. I was not at all sure I could bear the raw grief of these parents, nor did I feel equipped to handle an angry teenager demanding to know why this terrible thing was happening to her.

This alone would have made my visit difficult enough, but there was more. We social workers are taught in our training that our chief tool is our *self* – who we are, and how we relate to our clients. In this case, my self was bringing some major issues to the table. For one thing, I didn't happen to think much of Nurse Peggy myself – she struck me as rather young for hospice work, and rather task-oriented, without much warmth. For another thing, I was concerned about bridging the cultural

5

gap – the Hernandezes were Mexican-American, and I am not. I knew a thing or two that might be relevant – such as the significance of a 15-year-old girl dying when she should be celebrating her *quinceañera* – but I wasn't sure that that would suffice to help me connect with this family. And finally, I was eight months pregnant. Here I was, coming to help these parents who were past the age of childbearing, losing their only daughter, and I was going to waddle into their home looking like a pre-Colombian fecundity goddess. Fat chance they were going to relate to me. So I did the only thing I could think of to prepare myself for this experience: I breathed a quick prayer asking for wisdom and strength, and rang their doorbell.

I needn't have worried about being met at the door by anybody's raw emotion. Mr. and Mrs. Hernandez were polite, but cool. They answered my initial questions, but the body language was closed. I knew I wasn't connecting, so I changed course and asked to meet Graciela. No display of raw emotion here either – Graciela lay, pretty but comatose, on her bed. I was ashamed of the relief I felt as I realized that Graciela would not be challenging me with unanswerable questions. It was time for Mrs. Hernandez to administer a feeding into the tube in Graciela's stomach, and I sensed the slightest warming from the mother as she saw that I stayed at her side, watching the procedure with interest instead of excusing myself while she completed this task. I found myself shifting inwardly from an intellectual approach to an intuitive one, and I let myself just soak in the atmosphere around me. I was still a relatively-new social worker, and trusting my intuitions was not something I was accustomed to doing, but it felt right at this moment.

With the feeding completed, we adjourned back to the kitchen table. I began asking some more of my usual questions, trying to make this feel more like a conversation rather than an interrogation. As we sat there talking, a song started running through my head. It was "You Are My Sunshine". At first I ignored it, because it seemed ridiculous in this context, but it wouldn't go away. I began to feel very strongly that I was supposed to say something about it, even though I had no idea where this was leading, and I was certain that the parents would think I had completely lost my mind. Finally I blurted out, "This may sound really crazy to you, but this song, 'You Are My Sunshine', keeps going through my head here. I don't know why that is, but I just felt like I needed to share that with you." And I waited for one or the other of them to tell me that I was a lunatic, and that they would be calling my boss to have me fired. Instead, Mrs. Hernandez burst into tears, followed by Mr. Hernandez. Mrs. Hernandez looked at me like she was just now seeing me for the first time, and exclaimed, "That was her favorite song! On her first day of kindergarten, Graciela learned that song and she sang it around the house all the time!" That was when I started crying too.

After that, the pieces of the puzzle fell quickly into place. Peggy was a knowledgeable-enough nurse, but her examination of Graciela had been cursory, mechanical. Peggy did not have children of her own, and the Hernandezes felt that she did not truly understand what they were going through. They needed someone to see past their controlled, critical presentation to the agony within. When I "heard" their daughter's song – despite the disease, despite the passage of many years – they knew I could hear *them*.

This was to be my only meeting with the Hernandezes; Graciela died not long afterwards. But I learned two very important things that day: I learned to trust my inner voice as an important component of my professional repertory. And I learned that I had found my calling.

PART I
How Hospice Works

2
Hospice Then and Now

The word "hospice" comes from the same Latin word (*hospes*) that gives us the words "hospital" and "hospitality". The first hospices, in the Middle Ages, were monasteries where travelers spent the night. Those who were sick were attended to until they either recovered sufficiently to go on their way again, or died. The modern-day hospice was birthed in England, where Dame Cicely Saunders – a social worker and a physician – founded St. Christopher's Hospice in 1967.

In its earliest days in this country, there was the hospice *movement*. We were pioneers in uncharted territory. In 1976, the case of Karen Ann Quinlan was decided by the Supreme Court of New Jersey, allowing Karen's father to discontinue her ventilator after she had existed for some time in a persistent vegetative state due to a drug overdose. In 1990, the sad case of Nancy Cruzan was decided by the U.S. Supreme Court, affirming for the nation that decisional adults have the right to refuse medical/surgical interventions, and have the right to name a surrogate to make decisions on their behalf when they themselves cannot. The notion of a right to refuse treatment, and even of a right to die, was a grassroots movement that was thrashed out in numerous courtrooms; it paved the way for an equally-grassroots notion that people with terminal illnesses had the right to die comfortably in their own homes, surrounded by loved ones, rather than in hospital beds encumbered by medical paraphernalia and unwanted futile efforts at cure. Hospice's basic premise – that people should have the right to choose whether they want quality of life or quantity of life at its end – was a radical notion.

Now we have become the hospice *industry*. In some ways, our very success may be our undoing: as hospice – and its kissing cousin, palliative care – have become an accepted part of our healthcare system, we are increasingly scrutinized by Medicare and other regulatory bodies. In many areas, especially big cities, there is a highly-competitive atmosphere, with numerous hospice organizations fighting one another (*fighting?!*) for their fair share of the terminally-ill population. Hospice workers no longer march into the field with wholly altruistic motives. Our superiors urge us to be extra-friendly with the staff of "Bedside Manor" Nursing Home in hopes that the facility will refer more patients to us, and we are warned not to rock the boat despite the mediocre care provided by the "Pillhaven" chain of facilities, for fear that they will throw us out and give the referrals to another, less-critical, hospice. So I try to ignore the stench of Mrs. Smith's urine-soaked clothing, and smile as I oh-so-politely ask the nursing assistant if perhaps, when she has a moment, she could be so kind as to change Mrs. Smith's brief. (As a social worker, I am not *allowed* to do this in a nursing facility, because it is outside my scope of practice; otherwise I would do it myself, in a heartbeat.) Harder to ignore is our patient, Mrs. Washington, who has all her mental faculties, but is bedbound, without family or telephone, and who beseeches me at each visit to report the miserable nursing home where she resides to the state authorities. It is not as straightforward as one might think. The effectiveness of state agencies in dealing with nursing home transgressions is very questionable. I could report "Pillhaven" anonymously, but it would not take a rocket scientist to figure out that Mrs. Washington's only visitors are the hospice team members. The nursing home might then throw us out, the state agency might well accomplish nothing, and poor Mrs. Washington would have no visitors and even less care than she has now. *Ugh.*

The regulations that define hospice are numerous, but vague. Think of them as your minimum daily requirement for various vitamins and minerals. Certain basics are required in order to be a Medicare-certified hospice. Medicare reimburses hospices for care on a *per-capita, per-diem* basis. In other words, for each day that Mr. Goldstein is a hospice patient, that hospice receives a fixed daily sum, which is the same for all patients of all hospices in that geographical area. Hospices do not set their own fees, so there is no reason for patients or their families to comparison-shop on the basis of cost, because all the hospices in any given region are compelled to charge the same rates. The Medicare/Medicaid *per diem* may or may not actually cover the hospice's costs in delivering the care that Mr. Goldstein requires for his particular terminal illness. The expectation is that all those *per-capita, per-diem* amounts are aggregated into one giant pot of revenue, which is then used to pay staff salaries, office rent, expenses for medications and supplies, the laptops and cellphones used by the field staff, and all the other overhead and individual expenditures that make it possible for the hospice to provide care.

This leaves each hospice with a fair amount of discretion in what they do with the money, above and beyond those things that are mandated by the regulations. This is why one patient's experience with her local hospice may not bear any resemblance to that of her hairdresser's boyfriend's cousin who had hospice five years ago in another state. One hospice may decide to focus its efforts on providing comprehensive CNA (certified nursing assistant) coverage to all their patients. Another hospice may distinguish itself by offering art therapy, music therapy or massage therapy. One hospice may provide hospice-related medications at no charge, while another one assesses a $5 co-pay for all the medications it provides. One hospice may have primary nurses who are on-call for their own patients 24/7, while another uses a rotating team of nurses. Hospice X provides briefs, wet wipes and underpads to all its patients who need them, whereas Hospice Y provides only briefs. A hospice in a small town may have only a sole BSW social worker who provides very basic services to all their patients, while a hospice in a big city where MSW social workers are plentiful may have numerous social workers whose smaller caseloads and higher level of professional expertise allow them to provide more in-depth counseling services. To further complicate the picture, hospices with a generous philanthropic base may be able to provide additional services that are funded solely by donations. For those of you who are reading this book because you or someone you care about may be in need of hospice services, this may be very confusing. Give some thought to what really concerns you in your specific situation: Do you need a lot of assistance with your loved one's hands-on care? Are you worried that your relative will not reconcile with an estranged offspring before he dies? Are you confused by the many healthcare decisions you must make, and the differing opinions of various family members? Call your local hospice, and ask them to explain how they can help you with the issues that matter to you. If you are fortunate to live in an area where you have a choice among multiple hospice providers, talk to several of them and compare their answers. If your loved one resides in an assisted living or skilled nursing facility, ask the facility staff, and other families who have a loved one on a hospice program there, which one of the choices they prefer, and why. Chances are you will be able to discern which one is the best fit for your particular situation.

Not only are all hospices not the same, but all hospice *environments* are not the same, either. There is a world of difference between hospice in a small town or rural area where healthcare resources are often scarce, and hospice in a major metropolitan area where healthcare resources are plentiful, the atmosphere is highly competitive, and consumers are often very savvy. In a rural or semi-rural area, there is often only one hospice provider for the area, and often (but not always) its small size, and the relative lack of resources, may limit the services it can provide, and the circumstances under which it can provide them. (E.g., a rural hospice cannot offer music thanatology if there are no music thanatologists living anywhere in the vicinity.) By contrast, in the large metropolitan area where I lived and practiced, numerous for-profit and not-for-profit hospices compete, not only with one another, but with a diverse array of curative treatment options. For example, a cancer patient who has exhausted the gamut of conventional therapies may still have to decide whether to go the hospice route, to pursue any number of alternative/complementary medicine treatment possibilities, or to enroll in a clinical trial at one of the several major teaching hospitals in the area. If you add to this cornucopia of choices some distraught family members who are not altogether realistic about the patient's situation and prognosis, and who (with the best of intentions) cause the patient to feel like he or she is *hurting them* by being resigned to the prospect of his or her death, it is understandable that the pressure is intense. Often, when a person decides to enroll in hospice, it is after weeks or months of family discussion, or even pitched battles, about what the best course of action is. No wonder families come to us in shock and disarray.

The evolution of hospice paralleled a personal evolution for me. I began my hospice social work career in 1989. There were no laptop computers then. There were no cellphones then, and only the on-call nurse at night got to carry the bag phone – a primitive precursor to the cellphones we all now know and love. We had beepers, and when the boss wanted us, he entered his phone number, and we had to call back from the landline phone of whatever home we happened to be in, or find a payphone if we were driving. Documentation was done on paper, and turned in at the office once or twice a week for filing in each patient's chart by the secretary. When cellphones first became available, hospices were initially resistant to spend the money to provide them to staff; it would be several years before my employer figured out that the cost of cellphones and service would quickly be balanced out by the greater efficiency with which we could all do our jobs. (I once drove around for 45 minutes looking for a functioning payphone in a rundown neighborhood where most of the phones had been vandalized.) I finally learned to use a computer in 2000. This was a very stressful paradigm shift for most of the staff, and some of the older nurses decided that they would rather retire (or go to work somewhere else that did not – as yet – require computer competence) instead of learning this new skill.

Of course there was also an evolution of my own professional skillset. As I reflect back on some of these situations now, I am sometimes shocked at my own cluelessness. I was a reasonably bright 32-year-old woman with a master's degree, but I had very little practical experience. My one year of work at a family service agency had mostly been with middle-class Caucasians having first-world problems. I expected hospice patients to be dying, and I expected that they and their families would have challenges in coping with that situation. However, when I found myself confronted with destitution, homelessness, or elder abuse, I had no idea what I was supposed to do. Hospices in those early days were small. The one that hired me initially had no other social workers besides me – at least not in my first couple of years there – and the team managers were all nurses, so I had nobody to turn to for social work-specific guidance. I could not google the answers; there were as yet no online chatrooms wherein I could confer with more-experienced social workers. I learned a tremendous amount in those early years, often by messing up. I remember looking up various social service agencies in the Yellow Pages phonebook, calling them up, and asking them to explain to me what they did and how they did it. I went to my graduate school's library and read professional journal articles to fill in the lacunae in my knowledge. About four or five years into my career – by which time I had changed jobs and was now working with a hospice that had a whopping *four* social workers on staff – a solo social worker at another area hospice reached out to propose monthly get-togethers of all of us who were working in relative isolation for our respective employers. I was shocked to find out at this point that *I* was considered one of the more experienced ones!

3
Your Hospice, My Hospice

In any line of work, there is a constant tension between the perspective of the staff and the perspective of the customer. To the worker at the fast-food restaurant, yours is just one of several hundred burgers he will flip that day; to you, that burger is your lunch, and your hard-earned five bucks, and you want it *your* way: well-done, extra pickles, hold the mustard. The pinnacle of customer service is achieved when the burger-flipper makes you – the customer – feel like he genuinely shares your viewpoint, and cares as deeply as you do about whether you are satisfied with your cardio-patty.

How much larger does this loom when the commodity in question is not an inconsequential *nosh*, but the care provided to a loved one during their final days of life? It has been said that there are no do-overs in hospice. A hungry person can buy another burger elsewhere next time, but there is no next time for a loved one's final months of life. Raw emotions are so close to the surface, and the stakes are so high! But we – your loyal, but human, hospice workers – are subject to the same job stresses and strains as the guy behind the counter who puts the salt on French fries. We too have flat tires that make us late, sick children, budget constraints, crabby bosses, arguments with loved ones, and computers that crash – just to name a few.

Unlike Burger-Boy, however, we also have stressors that are unique – if not to hospice, then at least to healthcare. We really get attached to some of our patients and their families. We (I'm sorry to say) really *dislike* a few of the patients and families who come our way. But we must try our best to keep

19

those partialities hidden, and treat every person in accordance with their needs, not ours. Most of the time, I think we do this remarkably well. Sometimes, unfortunately, we fail at this crucial task, and I can only beg forgiveness, on behalf of all hospice staff everywhere, for the times when this happened, or may happen in the future.

In 2008, I changed jobs and agencies to return to the field as a hospice social worker, after seven years as a clinical manager of a hospice interdisciplinary team. A caseload of thirty to forty patients is large enough to force some juggling of conflicting priorities. None of those patients would want to hear (or feel, even if it is unsaid) that they are just one of thirty patients on my caseload. Their families wouldn't want to hear that either, and I certainly wouldn't blame them: each patient is an individual with a story that has brought them this far and (in most cases) with a group of people who are deeply affected by the fact that this individual is dying. So, when I go to meet with a new patient and family for the first time, I consciously take a few moments to center myself in mindfulness of the patient's perspective.

What am I there to do? From a Medicare standpoint, I am there to do the required psychosocial assessment on a new admission. Each core member of the hospice team – nurse, social worker, and chaplain – is required to do their own initial assessment on every patient admitted to our service. In the case of the social worker, this means finding out basic background information (marital status, ethnicity, religion, level of education, and so forth), who the family members are and how they are coping with the present situation, and what the patient knows about their illness and how they are dealing with it. We also need to know what the caregiving arrangements are, whether the patient has any advance directives, whether funeral plans have been thought out, and what other losses the patient or family members have experienced.

But I also realize that, from the patient's standpoint, I am just one of a half-dozen or so new faces that have come barging into the house since they signed those consent forms for hospice. I know that the idea of being assessed by a social worker gives most people the creeps, so I don't use that word when speaking to families. Usually what I say is something along the lines of, "I'd like to come over and introduce myself, get acquainted with you folks, and see how I can help out."

Once I'm in the home, I try to keep it real. I don't whip out my laptop (though I carry one in my tote bag), start firing questions and furiously jot down notes. Instead, my approach is just to get a conversation going, listen and observe intently, and gently steer the discussion toward the things I need to know. This almost always works well – I get the information I need, and the family doesn't feel like they've been involuntarily psychoanalyzed. But I'm not saying this is the only right way to do it. It's the way that works for me, and other social workers may go about their assignments differently. It's how I balance *my* need to meet the Medicare requirements for social work with *the patient's* need to check out and establish rapport with these new people who are barging into their home.

I often tell families that the social worker's role is multifaceted. First, I'm there to gather real human information about the real human being who is our patient. The healthcare system has a way of quickly reducing people to little more than their diagnoses – a middle-aged husband and father goes to the ER with severe abdominal pain, and two hours later overhears himself being referred to by one of the docs as "the appendix in room 7". When the illness is terminal, weeks or months of wrangling with the medical establishment can leave a person feeling that their entire life has been redefined by this macabre dance with disease.

Hospice is a holistic type of care, and to help restore a sense of wholeness to the person, we must know something about who that person was before disease moved in and stole their identity. So I absorb as much as I can about our new patient, which allows me to convey to the rest of the team some flavor of the human being who happens to have this diagnosis. Some of this I learn from what the patient and family tell me about themselves, but much of it is also gleaned from simply paying attention with all my senses and my intuition. Does an extensive gallery of family photos line both sides of the hallway? Probably this is a close-knit group to whom family ties are very important. Is the home large and exquisitely decorated? Small and run-down? Cozy but immaculate? I discern something about the family's financial status, and also their priorities. Do the family members sit with controlled dignity as they recount their story? Or is it bedlam, with people contradicting one another, children continually interrupting, and pets taking the scenic tour of everyone's lap? This will reveal – more than what anyone tells me – what the family dynamics are like, and how the family deals with strong emotions. We are not there to judge anyone. All this knowledge helps us tailor the hospice services to the patient's and family's end-of-life goals.

Another facet of the social worker's role is to provide information to the patient and family. Do they need to hire a caregiver or find a nursing home? I have lists, and can educate the family on how to go about this. Does the patient want to designate someone as power-of-attorney for healthcare? I have the appropriate forms right here in my tote bag. Are they looking for a dentist or podiatrist or hairdresser who will make a house call? I have names and phone numbers of several.

Finally, although I am not in a position to provide in-depth long-term psychotherapy to a caseload of thirty to forty patients, plus all their family members, I can certainly provide short-term counseling where requested: to help families say the things they need to say to one another, to help them solve current problems or start to heal old wounds, or simply to help them articulate and explore the diverse emotions that can be stirred up by having a terminal illness take up residence among them.

The psychosocial plan of care – another Medicare requirement – evolves out of this initial conversation. Some families may want the social worker to visit weekly to provide support. Others may identify discrete tasks with which they want assistance, and will want the social worker to visit only until those specific problems are resolved. Still others have no clearly-defined goals for social work involvement, but appreciate an occasional phone call or visit just to check in. Hospices may differ in the professional qualifications they require of their social work staff, as well as the caseloads the social workers are expected to carry, but these general roles apply to hospice social workers everywhere.

The other members of the hospice team, meanwhile, are doing the same thing in their respective disciplines. When a patient first elects hospice, the nurse and chaplain will also call to introduce themselves, and to schedule their initial assessment visits. Other services – such as volunteers or various therapies – may be offered if available and appropriate. Sometimes patients or family members complain of feeling somewhat overwhelmed, during that first week or so, by all the new people who want to come over.

But it is important to understand that our purpose is to learn as much as possible about each new patient and each new situation, so that we can best accommodate that unique set of circumstances and goals. It is never our intent to be nosy, judgmental or overwhelming. Our intent is to get the information we need in order to best help each patient. We want all our patients to have hospice their way.

4

Hospice is Not a Place

When Dame Cicely Saunders founded St. Christopher's Hospice in London, in 1967, the modern hospice movement was born. However, when hospice philosophy traveled across the pond, the model of service delivery needed to change. The United States is a land of wide-open spaces (even now), and gathering the terminally ill in "hospice houses" was not practical for much of the country. Also, there was a lot of grassroots support for allowing people to die in the comfort of their own homes, rather than in institutions (no matter how lovely they might be). So the original concept of hospice in the U.S. was care that was provided by an interdisciplinary team that would come to people's homes.

Ironically, we have come full circle about where and how to deliver hospice care. Many elderly people reside in nursing homes or assisted-living communities; these are their "homes", so it made sense to allow hospices to provide services in those facilities. Sometimes a hospice patient – despite the best efforts of the team – may develop a symptom that simply cannot be managed at home, and the person needs to be hospitalized for a few days to get the situation back under control. Hospices realized that it made sense to develop contractual relationships with their local hospitals in order to provide GIP (general inpatient) care focused on palliation of symptoms rather than curative treatment. It was only a short step from this to the realization that hospices could build their own GIP facilities (usually referred to as inpatient units, or IPUs). Since these were not full-fledged hospitals that would require operating rooms, X-ray machines, ICUs, etc., it was possible to create beautiful inviting patient rooms large enough to accommodate visiting friends and family, as well as calm spaces like chapels and gardens where people could go to center themselves. These IPUs are staffed by hospice employees trained in palliative care, so the necessary expertise is on hand 24/7. The basic model of hospice is still services provided in the home, but hospice has been able to address the needs of many more people because of the different levels and locations of care that are now available.

When I first began working in this field, I assumed that I would be visiting my patients and their families in the patients' homes, and indeed this was true most of the time. But sometimes family members wanted to meet me elsewhere – perhaps because they wanted to discuss something but not in front of the patient, perhaps because they didn't want the patient to know that they were meeting with the social worker, or perhaps simply because they didn't live near the patient's house and wanted a more convenient location. Working family members sometimes could not take time off of work to meet with me, which is how I found myself brown-bagging it one day at a car dealership with a patient's daughter who worked there. I conducted a family conference at Gojo's Café in Waukegan, and many other family meetings at diverse Starbucks locations. Another dutiful daughter spent several hours every day sitting at her mother's bedside in a nursing home, but when she wanted to complain to me about the facility, I sat with her on a stretch of curb bordering the parking lot so that we could enjoy some fresh air and sunshine together, and talk without being overheard by the facility staff.

Mrs. Gladstone was a hospice patient with end stage dementia, residing in a suburban nursing home. It was one of those facilities where the staff was (for the most part) devoted, and tried hard, but it was primarily Medicaid, meaning there just weren't a lot of dollars for the staff to work with. So Mrs. Gladstone's care was marginally adequate, but not necessarily what you would ideally want for your mother. Her daughter, Amanda, was not happy about the situation, but was not in a position to pay for a better nursing home. I advocated for her with the facility staff, trying to get them to be a bit more attentive to details, but there was no dramatic improvement. Amanda felt stuck, and needed someone to complain to. I agreed to come to her home so that we could speak freely without fear of eavesdroppers.

Amanda had a nice home, which she shared with two enormous Great Danes. Full disclosure: I am a cat person, and have no affection for huge dogs. However, Amanda promised me that she would have them confined for my visit. "Confined" turned out to mean that she had stretched a baby gate across the opening between the living room and the kitchen; we sat at the kitchen table, while the dogs watched us intently and longingly from a few feet away, behind an obstruction that they could easily have just stepped over. As Amanda and I talked, the dogs grew increasingly unhappy about not being allowed to come investigate the new person (me) who was in their space. Amanda asked me if she might let them out. She assured me that they were gentle giants who only wanted to sniff me. I wasn't happy about this, but I felt that I had no right to tell her that she had to make her pets miserable in their own home for my sake, so out they came. First one giant, and then the other, came over to check me out. With me seated in a chair, their heads were above mine, and I felt hot doggy breath in my ear. When one of them looked like he might lick me, I turned my face aside to dodge the gesture, but otherwise just sat as motionless as possible.

I think Amanda took pity on me at last, because after a few minutes, she made them return to their incarceration in the living room. Then she looked at me for a moment and said, "Don't move...." Since the dogs were already confined, I couldn't imagine what further threat might be lurking, but I did as instructed. She grabbed a handful of paper towels, then came over to me and tenderly removed about a cup of gelatinous Great Dane saliva from the shoulder of my blazer. *Yuck!*

5
Language Matters

Hospice patients *die*. They do not "pass away", "transition", "perish", or "expire". Driver licenses expire. Cartons of milk expire. Human beings *die*. As you read this, did you cringe a little? One of the things that hospice workers can do is model the use of reality-based language. We are not harsh or uncaring, nor are we ignorant of the many cultural norms that exist. We are trying to help you – the family member – come to terms with what is happening. Many cultural groups have a real taboo about the use of direct language in these situations. I usually get my first clue during my initial assessment, when one of the family says something like, "Are you going to be here when … uh … when something happens with Mom?" This is a very delicate moment, because I want to answer the question, but I also want to (gently) expose that phrase "when something happens" for the icky little euphemism that it is. I need to model for the family that one can use the proper, grown-up word for death without anything terrible happening.

Another way that language looms large is the use (or non-use) of medical jargon. Of course some of our patients have a relative who is a doctor or nurse, but the vast majority of the family members we work with are not healthcare professionals. Part of my responsibility as a hospice social worker is to translate medical jargon into plain English. "Getting fed through a tube" is more comprehensible to the average person than the acronym "TPN" or the term "PEG tube". "Tumor" is more understandable than "neoplasm". "Do you want paramedics to try to restart Dad's heart when he dies?" makes more sense than "Is he a DNR?" Sadly, some physicians have a very hard time speaking the truth to their patients, so they say things like, "When you get stronger, we can do some more chemotherapy," when they know full well that the patient has little-to-no chance of doing anything other than declining. So sometimes I am not only translating medical jargon, I am also cautiously providing insight into the doctor's own denial.

As I try to establish and maintain a rapport with the patient and her family, I look for clues about who they are in the language they use about *non*-hospice issues also. Many times the TV news may be on, and we find ourselves chatting briefly about current events. Do they label those protestors outside a clinic as "anti-abortion" or "pro-life"? Do they refer to the formal recognition of a same-sex union as "gay marriage" or "marriage equality"? I keep my ears wide open for those revealing details, to better understand who this family is.

The language that we hospice staffers use in our documentation is also extremely important. It is always better to use objective descriptors than subjective labels. What one person considers a messy house may seem quite normal to another observer. But if I say that there is a large pile of dirty dishes in the sink, and dog feces in multiple locations on the carpeting, the reader gets a much clearer picture of the conditions. It is better to say that the patient "has a history of opiate drug abuse" than to brand him "an addict". I may feel that the patient's son is an arrogant jerk, but I will chart something along the lines of, "The patient's son is a rheumatologist, and voiced strong opinions regarding his mother's plan of care." We can never forget that a patient may at some point request a copy of his hospice chart, or that circumstances may lead to our documentation being read aloud in a courtroom. (That doesn't have to be the result of any wrongdoing by the hospice, by the way. One patient's son filed a lawsuit against his late mother's nursing home, alleging inadequate care; our hospice documentation was subpoenaed for the purpose of demonstrating that the hospice staff did a *great* job providing care, while the nursing home staff dropped the ball repeatedly.) The language with which we document can also reflect the presence or absence of critical thinking on our part. For example, do I chart that the patient is "noncompliant with medications", or do I write something that reflects my thoughtful exploration of the issues? "The patient stated she is worried about becoming addicted to morphine if she takes it for pain" demonstrates that I took the time to find out *why* she is noncompliant; now her plan of care logically includes some education to address her concerns.

Language both *reflects* our thought processes and *shapes* them. The patient's and family's choice of words communicates a great deal to the hospice team about who they are and what they need from us. And our choice of words reveals whether we see our patients and families as problems to be solved, or human beings going through a very human situation.

6

Pain Management and the Role of the Social Worker

Family members – if they know anything at all about hospice – know that we are there to help their loved one (a) stay out of the hospital as much as possible, and (b) die comfortably. But what does dying comfortably mean? And who gets to define that term? It's not as simple as you might think.

Pain is an inherently subjective experience. If I come upon a person screaming, and I see a bloody bullet wound in the person's leg, it would be reasonable for me to assume that this person is in severe pain. But perhaps he is screaming in fear, not pain. Perhaps she is a participant in a disaster response exercise, and the bullet hole is actually an expert make-up job. Perhaps he is only slightly wounded, but exaggerating the injury in order to elicit his girlfriend's sympathy. No matter how much I may want to, I cannot actually know what that person is experiencing.

A thermometer can tell me objectively what someone's temperature is. A blood pressure cuff can tell me objectively what the individual's blood pressure is. But there is no "pain-o-meter" to objectively measure a person's level of pain. In an effort to impart some degree of objectivity, medical practitioners often ask patients to describe their pain using a 0-10 scale, with 0 being no pain at all, and 10 being the worst pain imaginable (on par with passing a kidney stone, or unmedicated childbirth). The goal is to make pain control *measurable*: for example, if a person says his pain is "8", then takes pain medication and an hour later reports his pain is now "2", that particular dose of that particular pain medication appears to be very effective at controlling his pain. The hospice perspective is that pain is what the patient says it is. However, unlike objective measurements, self-reports may be swayed by other factors.

Enter family dynamics. The old man says that his cancer pain is a "6", and he doesn't want to take any medication for it because it makes him "loopy". He says he can just put up with the pain. His granddaughter informs his hospice team that Grandpa is a World War II veteran who experienced terrible things in combat; he is stoic by nature, but she really wants him to be pain-free in his final weeks of life. Grandpa dismisses her comments, but remarks that "better men than me toughed it out in the foxholes" when they were grievously wounded. He refers to the morphine proffered by the hospice nurse as "dope", and wants nothing to do with it. It is clear to me that Grandpa equates "toughing it out" with nobility of character, and "taking dope" with both physical and moral weakness. My job is to help grandfather and granddaughter reach some sort of compromise that reassures her, while also respecting his wish to feel that he is going out with his pride and dignity intact.

Another scenario. An elderly woman has been living with Parkinson's Disease for over twenty years, and it has now reached a terminal stage where she is nearly bedbound, and having difficulty swallowing. She complains constantly of spasms in her legs and feet, and random stabbing pains in various parts of her body. When asked to rate her pain, she often rolls her eyes and tells us that on a 0-10 scale, "it's a 14". Some pain medications appear to produce no benefit at all, others work briefly but wear off too quickly, and others make her sleep too much of the time. She states that she cannot stay focused when I try to lead her in a guided relaxation. The most effective interventions seem to be non-pharmacological: all the members of the hospice team spend time massaging her legs, feet, neck, and shoulders when we visit. Her adult children live in the area, but rarely visit; when I speak with one of the daughters, she says that Mom has always been a drama queen, and she (the daughter) is tired of it. To me, it looks like Mom is highly narcissistic, and uses the inherent subjectivity of her symptoms to manipulate everyone around her into giving her more time and attention than she would otherwise get. My role here is to help both the team and the family to set limits (lovingly) with this patient. It is much easier to give her full attention once it has been made clear that the visit will have a predetermined finite length.

These are just two examples of how intra- and interpersonal factors can impact the hospice team's ability to make our patient comfortable. Families sometimes get upset when they feel that the hospice nurse is providing either too much or too little pain medication, because their understanding of their loved one's level of pain is different than what the patient himself is reporting. While the hospice nurse is tasked with trying different medications until arriving at the right one and the right dose, the hospice social worker (and often the hospice chaplain as well) are tasked with sorting out what other issues are interfering with effective pain management, whether the real pain may actually be emotional or spiritual more than physical, and what the word "comfortable" means both to the patient and to her caretakers.

7
Hospice Mythology

Much of what a hospice social worker (or nurse, or chaplain, or any other team member) does on a daily basis is not taught in school. I went to an excellent graduate school of social work, but there was no class on how to tell an anxious daughter that her mother is probably going to die in the next 24 hours, or how to appear confident when changing an adult's diaper because there's nobody else around to do it. Most hospices spend a lot of time and energy orienting new staff to their positions – not only classroom time, but also time shadowing more experienced team members out in the field. Part of this orientation involves learning how to respond to tough questions and tough situations. For example, physician and nursing training teaches a healthy fear of morphine and other opiate drugs: they are addictive, and can cause respiratory depression. Family members (who may be medical professionals themselves) are often concerned about the seemingly wanton use of these heavy-hitting medications in hospice. Sometimes we are even accused of trying to kill their loved one. So we are taught to explain how morphine is used differently in the context of hospice (to avoid addiction and respiratory depression), and how it really is often the most effective drug to manage the pain of terminal cancer. Collectively, I have come to refer to this body of hospice-specific knowledge as "hospice mythology", and most of it is very valuable.

However – and this is where I have to call out many fine people that I've worked with over the years – some hospice mythology is just plain bullcrap. Three examples come to mind:

1) "You have to give her *permission* to die." This originates from a legitimate observation: on occasion, a dying person seems to hang on because of some unresolved family situation, such as a spouse or adult child who is very dependent on the patient. The dying person is worried about how that family member will cope with the death, and in some instances, appears greatly relieved if that family member can say, "Of course I am terribly sad and don't want to lose you, but I *will* survive, just as I would want you to go on if I were the one dying." But sometimes the concern is entirely justified, and it is clear to everyone that the soon-to-be bereaved family member has significant mental health issues that leave real doubts about his coping ability and possibly even about his ability to survive. In that situation, it is simply cruel for others to keep pressuring that individual to give permission when it would very obviously be insincere. The focus instead needs to be on providing reassurance to the patient that she has done everything that could be done to help her family member, and letting her know what supports are in place for this family member before and after the death.

The permission-to-die idea can also backfire. Back when I was a very new social worker, I worked with Mrs. Sardini and her husband. Mrs. Sardini was in the terminal phase of a long-term chronic condition, and the elderly Mr. Sardini was wearing thin. He had a lively sense of humor, and kept up a good front, but the situation was clearly grinding him down, even though there were hired caregivers in place to provide her physical care. He was able to acknowledge that he was ready for her ordeal (and his own) to be over. Somewhere along the line, some well-intentioned person told Mr. Sardini that he needed to give his wife permission to die, and then she would be able to "let go". I asked him, after the fact, how this conversation had gone. Mr. Sardini heaved a sigh as he replied, "I told her that it was OK for her to die. She raised up on one elbow, looked at me, and asked, 'Is it OK if I live?'" *Ouch.*

2) "He just had to get comfortable so that he could die." This is sometimes said by hospice nurses when they are talking to a family member who may have been somewhat ambivalent about their loved one receiving strong pain medication. I'm sorry, but this is nonsense, and in my opinion, it primarily serves the nurse's own need for reassurance about using such medications. People have been dying uncomfortably since the dawn of time – from prehistoric maulings by sabretooth tigers, to present-day deaths in car accidents, gun violence, or fires. We hospice workers want our patients to be comfortable because that increases their quality of life, not because comfort enables them to die.

3) "Unfinished business". Again, there is a grain of truth in this. If a patient seems to be lingering longer than expected in their final dying process, a hospice team member may ask if it is possible that he has some unfinished business that needs to be resolved in order for him to die. Certainly in some

instances, this is absolutely the case: I watched a dying mother hang on for nearly a week while I worked with the Red Cross to get her soldier son sent home from his overseas deployment, and she died within half an hour of his arrival at her bedside. But I have watched family members sometimes torment themselves trying to figure out what possible unfinished business Grandma might have, when in all likelihood her body is simply following its own internal timetable. Which brings us to the next topic....

8
It's Not Like You See in the Movies

For the vast majority of human history, people were all-too-well acquainted with the reality of death and dying. There was nowhere to go to avoid it. Even as recently as 100 years ago, most people in Western countries did their birthing and dying in their own homes, attended by family members, and this is still the case in other parts of the world. People kept domesticated animals that were born and eventually died in the house or barn. The average human lifespan was far less than it is nowadays, and infant mortality was higher. So virtually everyone, by the time they reached adulthood, had had some firsthand experience seeing both humans and animals dying. But in our modern era – with longer lifespans, and with hospitals and nursing homes assuming much of the physical care of the ill and elderly – it is possible to reach the age of 50 or 60 without ever having experienced the loss of a loved one, let alone actually watching someone die. So where do we get our information? From Hollywood.

I will not name specific movies or programs here, but if you have ever watched a film or TV show about someone who dies of a terminal illness, you "know" certain things that just aren't true:

    1) In the movies, nobody lingers in their final actively-dying days. Remember that the story has to play out in ninety minutes (or less, if it's a TV program), so there is no time to show the protagonist lying in bed for a couple of weeks in a comatose or semi-comatose state. In real life,

however, each body has its own internal timetable, which can be affected by many factors such as the diagnosis, whether or not the person has been recently given intravenous fluids or feedings, the person's overall condition, and their will to live (or lack thereof). This gives rise to concerns about unfinished business, if the family has not been advised to expect this reality.

2) In the movies, the dying person looks way too good. They may be slightly pale, or a little skinny, but basically they look like themselves. Keep in mind that these are *actors*. In real life, the dying person – if he has been ill for any length of time – probably looks pretty bad. He may be skeletally thin. Her hair is disheveled, the artificial color has all grown out and the grey is revealed, and she hasn't been tweezing those wild hairs on her chin. His dentures no longer fit, so he is toothless. Her complexion may be pale, or yellowish, or greyish.

3) In the movies, dying people are generally interactive almost up to the very end. They speak slowly, softly, but cogently, until they lie back on their pillow, close their eyes, and take a final breath. In real life, this is rarely the case. People are often unresponsive for hours, days, or even weeks prior to death.

4) In the movies, dying people tie up all the loose ends: they receive forgiveness for a past wrongdoing, they finally share their true feelings to someone, or they reveal a family secret that explains all the rest of the movie's plot. In real life, not so much. I won't say it *never* happens, but in my experience, either there were no loose ends to

begin with, or the dying person took those loose ends to the grave with him.

5) In the movies, family members sit around having Meaningful Conversations: they tell the dying person how much they love her, they read her favorite poems aloud, or they talk with her about the details she wants for her funeral or memorial service. In soap operas, they huddle in the hallway, conniving about who will wrest control of the family business once Dad dies. In real life, those things do happen sometimes, but in many cases, the bedside discussions are much more mundane: they debate whether to order pizza or Chinese food for dinner, they wonder why Dad's feet are purple and why his breath stinks, or they talk about things that have nothing to do with the person lying in the bed a few feet away. In my experience, those families were usually happy to see me when I would stop by, because I could assure them that it was normal and OK *not* to be having Meaningful Conversations, and because I could introduce new topics of conversation ("Tell me a Dad story....")

PART II
Evolving

9

First Time Seeing a Patient Die

The layperson probably assumes that hospice workers see patients die every day. The reality, however, is that our visits occupy only a very small percentage of any given patient's day, so we don't actually witness the precise moment of death as often as you might think. Nurses are, of course, the likeliest ones to be present for the last breath, because that is who the family usually wants to see when they think the moment is at hand. But each dying person has his or her individual internal timetable, and may die before the nurse gets there, or after the nurse has left. I have known team members from other (non-nursing) disciplines who have worked in hospice for a year or longer without ever having seen a patient die.

I had been dispatched to do my psychosocial assessment on Mr. Rivera, an elderly resident of a nursing home that specialized in dementia care. I sat at the bedside with Mr. Rivera's middle-aged son, Daniel, gathering information in my typical low-key way, while Mr. Rivera lay quietly in an unresponsive state in his narrow hospital bed, in the small and stark private room. He had had advanced dementia for a long time already, and Daniel was clearly very prepared for the death, whenever it might come. I was too green at that stage to make my own assessment of a patient's prognosis, and nobody had told me that Mr. Rivera might be dying imminently. But, somewhere in the course of conversation, I happened to glance over at Mr. Rivera and noticed that he did not appear to be breathing. I told Daniel that I thought his father had just died, and he seemed to take this news in stride. This was the first time I had actually been present when death occurred, and I think I was more shaken up than the son was – not because the patient had died, but because the departure of his soul from his body had taken place unnoticed and without fanfare. Somehow I had expected the event to call attention to itself in some fashion – perhaps a sigh, or some subtle change in the atmosphere of the room that a sensitive person might attune to. But there was nothing -- at least not that I was aware of.

I rang for the staff nurse, and told her that I thought Mr. Rivera had just died. She put her stethoscope to his chest, listened for a moment, and then, to my surprise, burst into tears. One of the things that has kept hospice work so fresh for me all these years is the fact that there are so many surprises. It is a constant, much-needed, reminder to me to go with the flow and not bring too many of my own expectations to each encounter. The nurse quickly regained her composure, and briefly shared with us the reason for her tears: she had come to work at this particular facility because she really enjoyed older people. At a dementia-focused nursing home, she expected that she would establish long-term relationships with her patients, unlike at other nursing homes where the focus was on acute care and rehabilitation. This facility had been open only a few months, and she had not really spent any time anticipating how patient deaths in the context of those long-term relationships would affect her. Although a few other patients had become acutely ill and ended up dying in the hospital, Mr. Rivera was the first resident who had actually died right there in the nursing home. It was so interesting to me that, at my first hospice death, the family did not have much need for my support, but the nurse did. I was glad, for her sake, that she could allow herself to drop the professional mask for a few minutes and just be the real, caring human being that she obviously was.

10
"Fittin' to die"

That was how Annie, one of the first hospice CNAs I worked with, described our patient. I was still pretty new at this hospice stuff. We were seated at our weekly interdisciplinary team (IDT) meeting, where all the disciplines met to discuss our patients and develop their plans of care. Because some team members were more talkative by nature, and some more reticent, our team manager Marcia had decided that she would simply call on us one at a time; that way, nobody got to dominate the conversation, and nobody could escape contributing.

We were discussing Mr. Parker. The nurse reported that his urinary output was decreased, as was his appetite. However, he was not in any severe pain, nor was he in respiratory distress. She detailed the medication adjustments she had made in the past week. The chaplain reported that Mr. Parker was a Methodist, and that the pastor from his church had recently visited to offer support. I was one of the team members who (at that point in my professional evolution) was inclined to say as little as possible; I don't recall what I said, but I'm sure it was as brief as I could get away with.

Then Marcia called on Annie, who was a woman of few words. She had been a CNA for many years. While not a highly educated woman, Annie had a tremendous amount of practical wisdom, the value of which she regularly underestimated. If she could have made herself invisible in the IDT meeting, she surely would have. But Marcia genuinely wanted to hear what Annie had to say, and coaxed her to share her assessment.

"He fittin' to die," Annie said tersely. "Tell us more about that," Marcia encouraged. "His nose has gone pointy and his ears is laid back," Annie elaborated. After that, no more words could be cajoled out of her. She had said all that she felt needed to be said on the matter.

I, the newbie, pondered those words in my heart. The nurse had talked about Mr. Parker's various bodily systems and vital signs, but Annie's down-to-earth report had cut right to the meat of the matter: Mr. Parker was on the brink of death. But what was this business about his nose going pointy and his ears laying back? I was mystified what this could mean, and resolved that I needed to gain a better understanding of this gem of folk wisdom.

When a family has a loved one in hospice, it is natural that they want to know exactly when death might occur. They have reservations to go on a cruise in two months – should they cancel their plans? One of the adult children lives in Europe and needs to know how soon she should fly in. If mom is only going to live another week or so, the family members feel they can manage her care themselves, but if this is going to go on for a month or more, they probably need to hire caregivers. I had heard hospice nurses discuss prognoses with families in only the most general terms ("I wish I had a crystal ball…"), not wanting to get it terribly wrong in either direction. This was the first time I had heard a coworker state with such certainty that she *knew* when this patient was going to die. How did she know?

There followed many conversations with Annie and other CNAs, as well as my own observations. What I came to understand is that what Annie described (and experienced CNAs all know) are signs of advanced dehydration – the kind that results when patients are so close to death that their bodies are no longer capable of properly utilizing water. Our skin normally contains a lot of liquid, and when dehydration occurs, the facial skin appears to recede, causing the eyes to look sunken, and the nose to look more prominent. Our earlobes are particularly juicy. Just give your own a squeeze as you read these words, and notice that they feel spongy. But when a dying person is very dehydrated, and they are lying on their back in bed, the earlobes are wrinkly, and "lay back" in folds, like window curtains. Once I had observed this phenomenon for myself, I took to pointing it out to family members who had questions about their loved one's prognosis, and for many of them it seemed to make more sense to them than arcane discussions about reduced urinary output.

The wisdom of CNAs, however, extends far beyond this. When people are physically naked and the CNA is performing the most intimate types of care, a certain degree of psychological nakedness often results as well. Patients will often share details of their lives with the CNA that they tell no one else. And because the CNA is with the patient more frequently, and often for longer periods of time, than the other disciplines, he or she has a lot of opportunity to observe what goes on in the household. I cannot count the number of times that a team CNA told me, "You know the grandson is stealing her meds, right?" or "That daughter beats her kids," or "His caregiver is bringing our diapers to her grandmother – that's why she's always asking us for more."

If you want to know what's really going on with a patient, ask the CNA.

11
Touching a Dead Person for the First Time

I was headed to the home of new patient Mrs. Peterson, to do my initial psychosocial assessment. When I entered the lobby of the apartment building, I was surprised to find one of the hospice nurses already there ringing the buzzer. I asked why she was there, and she informed me that Mrs. Peterson had just died. This was before cellphones, so the office could not reach us out in the field except via our beepers. The nurse was very glad to see me, because my presence meant that she could quickly do her task of confirming the absence of vital signs, and then move on, leaving *me* there for the more time-consuming business of providing emotional support to the bereaved family members.

Mrs. Peterson was indeed dead, and having established this fact, the nurse made the necessary phone calls, and promptly left. I remained at the bedside with Mrs. Peterson's daughter and niece, providing support while we waited for the funeral director to arrive. Although they had not expected her to die at that particular moment, they had had a lot of time during her illness to prepare themselves, so they were not inordinately grief-stricken. Our protocol for deaths was that some member of the hospice team was to stay with the family until the funeral home staff picked up the patient's body, so I settled into an overstuffed chair, and encouraged the two women to reminisce about their mother and aunt. After some conversation along these lines, it became apparent that the daughter had something else on her mind, and she was having some difficulty expressing it. "Could you, um…. My mother wanted me to, uh, have her necklace…." For a brief moment, I failed to grasp the real significance of her words. Then, as I followed the daughter's gaze, I saw that the necklace in question was around Mrs. Peterson's neck. Mrs. Peterson's *dead* neck. Mrs. Peterson's daughter was clearly afraid of touching her dead mother, but she wanted the necklace, and she wanted *me* – the hospice professional, who of course should be very comfortable with this – to remove said necklace from her mother's cold dead skin.

I had been a hospice social worker for perhaps a month at this point, and I had never *seen* a dead body up until this minute, let alone touched one. But two thoughts loomed very large in my mind. The first of these was not particularly noble: I didn't want to look like an idiot. The second thought was a more professional one: I knew, intellectually, that no harm was going to come to me from touching a dead person, and I felt it was my professional obligation to model this, to avoid reinforcing the daughter's fearfulness. So I took a deep breath, smiled and said, "Of course," and reached out to unclasp the necklace from Mrs. Peterson's neck. Lightning did not strike me dead. Mrs. Peterson's skin was somewhat cool, pale, and waxy-looking, but it still felt like skin. I handed the delicate little gold chain to the daughter with a feeling of accomplishment. It was one of many milestones in my growth as a hospice worker – Touching a Dead Person for the First Time. I saw the therapeutic power, for the family, of such a simple act, and from that moment onward, it became part of my routine when attending deaths always to find some reason to touch the deceased's body. Just a small act, perhaps, but it makes a strong statement that this person, although dead, is still a person, and death does not automatically change a loved one into something to be feared.

12
Death Means Different Things to Different People

Mrs. Rubin was in a nursing home, dying from a brain tumor. Most of our hospice patients – especially in nursing homes -- are elderly, but Mrs. Rubin was only 68 years old. Mr. Rubin was in his mid-seventies and physically unable to manage her care at home, but he visited her faithfully, several hours every day. I had been making weekly visits to provide emotional support, primarily to the husband. I had watched Mrs. Rubin grow less and less responsive over the past month, and she was now sleeping almost all the time. Mercifully, her diminished consciousness was her main symptom; she had not had any pain. (And, strange though it may seem to those who are not medical professionals, many patients with brain cancer never experience any pain from their tumors.) Her husband was, of course, grieving the loss of his partner, even though technically she had not yet died. But what concerned me most was his tremendous anxiety about what her death was going to be like. From the hospice team's perspective, Mrs. Rubin appeared comfortable, and we had every reason to expect that she would just quietly fade away. But no amount of reassurance sufficed to alleviate Mr. Rubin's apprehension that her death was going to be terrible.

One day, the end seemed to be quite near. I sat at the bedside with Mr. Rubin, and we talked quietly, somberly. I had deliberately arranged our chairs so that I could cast surreptitious glances at the rising and falling of Mrs. Rubin's chest, while making it difficult for Mr. Rubin to do the same.

Inhalation... exhalation... inhalation... exhalation.... No inhalation. I waited at least a minute, to be sure. The next breath never came. I reached over to touch Mr. Rubin's wizened hand, and said gently, "It's over." "That's it?" he questioned. "Yes," I said, "she's gone. I'll ring for the nurse." "That's *it*?!" he repeated, this time with his voice rising to emphasize the word "it". I again assured him that his wife had died, and that I would summon the facility nurse to verify this.

I did not expect the smile that broke across his face. He was astonished, relieved, even elated, that her passing had been such a non-event. And *then* he proceeded to tell me why. In all our previous conversations, he had never shared this story (and I was not yet experienced enough to know how to probe). When he was a young child, his mother had died of rectal cancer. (He was about six or seven at that time; doing the mental math, I estimated that this would have been in the early 1920s.) She died at home, and his recollection of her final days was that she had lain in bed, screaming and writhing in agony. This was the only death Mr. Rubin had actually seen, and at a very impressionable age. No wonder the poor man had believed, somewhere deep in his soul, that having cancer inevitably led to a tormented demise. In that moment when his wife peacefully departed from her body, he was finally able to free himself from the prison of that horrible childhood memory, and lay his beloved mother to rest at last. And for me, another hospice lesson learned: Always ask family members about their prior experiences with death and loss.

13
My Acting Career

I have never had any interest in acting as a career. I assiduously avoided speaking parts in all grade school plays, preferring to be a silent tree on stage, or better yet, behind the scenes as a painter of sets. No matter how many times I have stood at a lectern to address an audience, I still get stage-fright. But I have discovered that I have some acting ability when I have needed it most – not in front of a camera, but on that tiniest of stages, namely, a room full of hospice family members. People are panicking, or distraught, and suddenly all eyes are on *me*, The Hospice Professional, who is there to guide them through and to make everything OK. Their need draws out of me an ability to rise to the occasion, which I don't otherwise possess. At that moment, something inside me kicks into high gear, and I have discovered that I can *act* confident, and *act* like I know what I'm doing, even when that is far from the truth. That something is what made it possible for me to grasp the wrist of a newly-deceased woman and make a show of checking her pulse (even though I did not know at that time how to check a pulse), so that I could tell the disbelieving family at bedside definitively that yes, she was truly dead. That same something is what enabled me, at yet another death, to don rubber gloves and clean up the horrific mess generated by the deceased in her last moments, as if I did this all the time. The family's poignant need to have a better final image of their loved one far outweighed any personal feelings of fear or disgust on my part. I hope I have not spoiled anything for my readers by this revelation of fallibility and deception. This is why I said, back at the beginning of this book, that I could not say whether hospice workers truly are special people. It is true that we are, by and large, a compassionate group of folks. But we sneeze, fart, blush, make mistakes, arrive late, and feel unsure of ourselves at times, just like everyone else.

One of the things I learned very early on was to take a moment to center myself before every patient visit. Before getting out of my car, or before walking into the next room if I am seeing several patients in the same nursing home, I always pause briefly to take a few deep breaths and say a quick prayer asking God to use me as He sees fit in the upcoming encounter. This has freed me from any stage fright and the need to anticipate every possible turn of events that might occur, and every possible question that might be asked of me. I still won't do improv theater, but hospice work is perhaps improvisation at its finest.

14
Cultural Differences

As part of our educational process, social workers take classes in cultural sensitivity. In the context of hospice, it is very important to be aware that some ethnic groups speak very openly about death and dying, while in other groups, the subject is quite taboo. Different groups may have different modes of decision-making: typical American individualism stands in contrast to other groups where traditionally the male head of household makes decisions for the women, or where decisions are made more by group consensus. Pharmaceutical products may be eschewed in favor of prayer, herbs from the *curandera*, or complementary medicine. Many cultures are more receptive to assistance from one of their own, rather than someone who is perceived as an outsider. As a Jewish woman who "doesn't look Jewish" and doesn't have a typical Ashkenazi Jewish surname, I saw this latter point over and over with the Jewish families I worked with. My first visit sometimes felt rather constrained initially, but after I would drop a carefully placed *"Oy!"* or *"Mazel tov!"* into the conversation where appropriate, a family member would ask hopefully, "Oh, are you Jewish?", and the whole tenor of the interaction shifted noticeably. As I gained experience in my work, I learned always to be alert to these cultural details, which often impacted how our team would intervene in the patient's care.

Mrs. Radmilovich and her son Milan were Bosnian Serbs. They had recently immigrated to the United States after the Bosnian war and the break-up of the former Yugoslavia. They had been dirt-poor peasants who had nothing back in Bosnia, and they were no different here. She spoke no English, and her son, who worked sporadically as a mechanic, spoke broken English. The elderly Mrs. Radmilovich had end stage cardiac disease, and spent most of her time in bed. However, she had clearly been a force to be reckoned with in her life, and even now, when she told Milan (who was at least in his 40s) to jump, he asked how high. They lived in a ramshackle ancient wood-framed farmhouse in an unincorporated area of the county. A cat roamed around the house, and allowed me to scratch behind her ears, but when I tried to engage Milan in conversation about his pet, he seemed not to understand the concept: he tolerated the cat (and gave it the occasional table scrap) only because it controlled the mouse population that flourished in the fields surrounding the home. Although my encounters with them are now more than twenty years in the past, two things stand out in my memory. The first was that the cat – being an outdoor cat – eventually had kittens. I came to visit one day, and when I went to throw something out in the open kitchen garbage can, I was stunned to see inside it a pile of tiny, obviously dead, kittens. The Radmiloviches' barebones life left no room for sentimentality. Milan did not want to trip over them in the house, and did not want a growing population of feral cats on the property, so he simply strangled them and threw their little bodies in the trash. The second thing I recall vividly was that Mrs. Radmilovich – who no longer had the strength to walk to the bathroom – did her toileting in a large metal bucket next to her bed. The hospice nurse felt that it would be far more civilized to replace this with a bedside commode that had a proper seat and armrests, that could be cleaned more easily, and that the hospice would provide at no cost to her. However, Mrs. Radmilovich wanted no part of this contraption: through her son, she made it quite clear to the nurse that she had routinely peed and pooped in a bucket back in Bosnia, and it was good enough for her now as well.

15
The Disenfranchised

I began my hospice career in June, 1989. My notions of the work I was going to do, and the people I was going to do it with, were informed primarily by Elisabeth Kübler-Ross' books, and by the movie "Love Story". I had no idea that I was about to plummet headfirst down a rabbit hole populated by characters (some more sympathetic than others) who did not fit those idealistic narratives. Allow me to introduce three of them.

Carol: About a month into my first hospice job, I was assigned the case of Leon. I had a few demographic and medical details (53-year-old male with liver cancer), and an address, which I soon learned was a subsidized apartment building specifically designed to accommodate the low-income handicapped. Leon rolled up in a wheelchair to open his apartment door, because – as I quickly saw – he had a left leg above-knee amputation. He was wearing shorts, so his stump was visible, and he was not wearing his prosthesis. He was a stocky man, and his remaining limbs were surprisingly muscular. His face had a few days' growth of scraggly beard, and his greying hair and lined features made him look significantly older than his stated age. He was a bit gruff in demeanor, but allowed me in. I sat down on a couch, and he positioned his wheelchair a fair distance away from me. Wary, I thought. I had a hunch that he had had a hard-knock life, and was probably accustomed to social workers as a necessary evil. Our conversation – from my perspective – was bizarre. He answered my questions, but his body language betrayed him:

whenever I asked something he didn't really want to discuss, he rolled his wheelchair back a couple of feet. From the beginning, he pretty much took control of our interaction (I was a newbie), and talked mostly about what he wanted to talk about, which might or might not be responsive to my question. I felt like I was watching a very strange movie, and pretty much abandoned my efforts to elicit specific information, in favor of just letting him say what he wanted to say.

He was, I soon learned, a Vietnam veteran. He did not say – and I did not ask – whether that was where he had lost his leg. He informed me that, although his given name was Leon, he preferred for people to call him Carol. I don't think the word or the concept of "transgender" was widely known at that point, but it was clear that he was what in those days was called a "transvestite". (Note: I cringe now writing that word, but that was the terminology back in 1989.) While I had no formal information about any mental health issues he might have, I perceived a lot of paranoia in his thinking processes. Somewhere in the course of this initial visit, he mentioned that he supplemented his disability check by doing some babysitting for another woman in the building. As he said this, he nodded his head in the direction of another couch, and I saw for the first time that there was a small child sleeping under the blanket that was casually thrown there. As Leon/Carol talked about this child, he said that the boy had something wrong with his testicles and was going to need surgery. I was getting increasingly freaked out by this conversation, wondering if this child was in some way endangered by this care arrangement, and for that matter, whether *I* might be in danger. I realized that he had positioned himself between me and the only door to the apartment, but I calmed myself down by reminding myself that a one-legged person could probably not outmaneuver me. I somehow got through this initial meeting, and he was amenable to my visiting again. I went from this appointment over to a girlfriend's house, where I broke down in tears, feeling that I had made a horrible mistake by taking this job, because I obviously had no idea what I was doing!

The weekly hospice interdisciplinary team (IDT) meetings were a wonderful place for me to learn and grow. My coworkers had all been doing this work longer than me, and were very supportive and informative as I shared my observations and concerns. We agreed that we needed to respect this patient by calling her Carol, and using female pronouns, despite the fact that the physical body Carol inhabited was very much a male one. They felt that the childcare arrangement was not really a concern, because Carol was declining fairly rapidly and was soon unable to continue babysitting anyway. And it became apparent that, since Carol lived alone, she was going to need nursing home placement in the very near future.

This was going to be an interesting task, as Carol had no money, and therefore I was going to need to find a Medicaid facility that would be able to handle a large, paranoid, one-legged male Vietnam vet who identified as female. I decided this would have to be a face-to-face conversation, so I made an appointment with the administrator of the facility that I felt the most optimistic about, and explained the situation. To my pleasant surprise, he seemed very OK with and ready to take on this challenge. I informed Carol – whom by this time we had all grown rather fond of – and she was cautiously willing to go there. She didn't really have any other options. The hospice nurse made the transportation arrangements, and I made plans to visit a day or two after the transfer, to see how Carol was settling in.

I was not prepared for the sight that greeted me. Carol was sitting up in her hospital bed, wearing a lacy pink nightgown that had been provided by the nursing home staff. An abundance of chest hairs curled all around the straps and the neckline. Carol's face was clean-shaven, and her short hair washed and neatly combed. But – most importantly – for the first time that I had ever seen, she was smiling from ear to ear. I was so happy for her I almost hugged her.

Carol resided in that nursing home until her death several weeks later. During all the months that we had worked with her, neither our team nor the nursing home staff had been able to elicit any names of friends or family, and nobody except our team came to visit her in the home. Our team decided that, even though there was no money for anything beyond a Public Aid cremation, Carol deserved to be honored with a proper funeral. The funeral director was receptive, so the hospice nurse brought a bouquet of flowers, our team gathered to share our reminiscences about our time with Carol, and the team chaplain said some prayers. It was a beautiful send-off, at the end of a life that had probably seen very little beauty and far too much pain.

James: As I write this, I am holding on my lap one of my prized possessions – a limited-edition book of pencil sketches of nude men and women, signed by the artist. But it is not the book itself that is precious to me, but the memories of how I came to have it. The AIDS epidemic did not make it to the Midwest quite as quickly as it did to the major cities in California and New York. When I started my work in hospice, we folks in the heartland were just beginning to hear about AIDS. Nowadays, people can live many years with HIV infections held in control by medications, but in the early 1990s, it was a terrifying death sentence. James was a young gay man dying of AIDS. His partner and a cadre of other young gay men, many of whom were also infected, took care of him in his modest apartment. In those days, the gay community often rallied around whoever was sick with this new plague, and the hope was that others would in turn rally around them when their inevitable time came. Judgment and discrimination against gays (the term "LGBTQ" was not yet current) was widespread even before AIDS, and often even their own families had disowned them, so they took care of their own because there was no other choice.

James had been an artist of considerable success, and his artwork adorned the walls of his space. Now, however, he had developed AIDS-related dementia, and was highly confused. Somehow we bonded, though. He was fortunate to have an abundance of social and emotional support – well beyond any that I could have provided to him – but he enjoyed my visits, even though he was often unclear who exactly I was. Shortly before he died, his partner handed me a large book, wrapped in a white overlay, which was sealed with a sticker marking it as number 509/1000. "James wants you to have this," his partner told me. I carefully slid off the wrapping without breaking the seal, and my eyes filled with tears as I read what James had scrawled inside it. "For my sweetest brightest nurse (sic). You light up my life. Debbie Boone makes me sick. I love you." Beneath the scribbled writing was a cartoonish smiling face with dots for eyes and nose – such a far cry from the masterful sketches he had drawn for the book. What a loss that he – and so many other talented young people – died so prematurely from this terrible disease.

Lynn: Back in the early 1990s, Lynn and Marshall were a young couple in their 20s. They had been married less than a year, and had bought a starter home in a very conservative suburb. They were very sincerely religious Christians, and had both maintained their virginity prior to marriage. Neither of them had ever used any illicit drugs, nor gotten any blood transfusions. Yet Lynn was dying of AIDS. How could this have happened?

As it turned out, Marshall had been a virgin in only the most technical sense: he had indeed never had sexual intercourse with any woman before he and Lynn got married. However, in what he represented as an uncharacteristically impulsive moment, he had had a one-time sexual encounter with a *man*, a few weeks before the wedding. Unbeknownst to him, he was infected with HIV during that encounter. For whatever reason, Marshall did not develop any symptoms right away that would have caused him to seek medical care. In the sheltered world he inhabited, he might not even have been aware of AIDS, or how it was transmitted. Still asymptomatic, he got married, and promptly passed along the infection to his new wife, who knew nothing about his exposure or its circumstances. Tragically, she got sick very quickly. AIDS was just about the last possibility that anyone considered, but once it was conclusively diagnosed, the rest of the story had to come out.

Marshall and Lynn were both determined that nobody outside of the hospice team and Lynn's doctors could know what her diagnosis was. In those days, the stigma attached to AIDS was tremendous. And in the context of their conservative Christian beliefs and community, where AIDS was seen as God's wrath visited upon gays and drug abusers, it was even worse. Marshall still had only the mildest of symptoms, and was continuing to work; he was fearful that he would be fired if his employer learned that he had HIV. So Lynn's mother – who had been told that Lynn had cancer – assisted in Lynn's daily care while Marshall went to work, unaware of her daughter's true diagnosis. The hospice nurses did their best to impress upon the mother the importance of practicing universal precautions for infection control, but could not tell her the real reason *why* this was so important in Lynn's case.

Had they lived in the big city, there was a growing support network for "PWAs" (Persons With AIDS), but out in the suburban boondocks, there was absolutely nothing. But accessing such support – even if there had been any – would have required the willingness to acknowledge the diagnosis. I felt bad for Lynn, betrayed and effectively sentenced to death by the man she loved. I felt bad for Marshall who (I now realize) was probably grappling with homosexual feelings that caused him to question whether he should in fact get married; that "uncharacteristic" sexual encounter with a man may have been a desperate attempt to figure out once and for all whether he was gay or straight. He would have to live out his days knowing that he was the cause of his wife's death. But all our team also felt very angry at Marshall, whose dishonesty with himself and others had created this disaster, and kept his dying wife locked in a lie up to her final breath.

As I write these paragraphs, well into the 21st Century, I am exceedingly grateful that our society has made considerable progress in our understanding of gender and sexual orientation, and that these stories might play out quite differently if they were unfolding today.

16
Ethical Issues

It is one thing to take a class on bioethics. It is quite another thing to wrestle with these issues in real life. Over the course of my hospice career, I learned from many fine mentors, and from experience. Two cases – separated by at least 25 years – illustrate this process.

Very early in my hospice career, I met with Mr. Thorwald. His wife, who had just been admitted to our hospice, had had a major stroke months earlier. They were both in their mid-80s, and had no children. Mrs. Thorwald's stroke had knocked out her speaking and swallowing abilities, and she had had a feeding tube inserted. Because her husband could not possibly care for her at home, she had been placed in a nursing home, where he came daily to spend time with her. Now, Mrs. Thorwald was alert and somewhat interactive, sitting up in a wheelchair, but confused and unable to talk or make her own decisions; when I met her briefly, she smiled sweetly at me, but it did not appear to me that she comprehended the things I said to her. So most of the conversation was one-to-one with her husband, who explained his predicament to me.

Mr. Thorwald shared that, when his wife first had her stroke, he and her doctors were hopeful that she might recover to a significant degree. He had agreed to the feeding tube in order to support her through a trial of skilled rehabilitation. But she had made little progress, and her speech and her ability to swallow had not improved at all. Meanwhile, he had just been diagnosed with lung cancer, and had decided that he had lived long enough: he was not planning to pursue any treatment for himself. His goal in having his wife admitted to hospice was to discontinue her feeding tube, to ensure that she died before he did, because there were no other family members to visit her or to oversee her care.

I listened supportively to his story, and agreed that it was a very tough situation for both of them. Since Mrs. Thorwald had already been admitted to hospice, I had to assume that somebody somewhere in the organizational hierarchy felt that his plan was acceptable. Of course I kept my personal reaction to myself, but I was very troubled by this. Back at the office, I spoke to my team manager very frankly: from my perspective, this woman was not actually terminally ill, and her husband – whatever his motivation – wanted to kill his alert and smiling wife by stopping her tube feedings. I told my boss that I was going to have to withdraw from this case on ethical grounds, and he would need to assign a different social worker. He did, so I had no further information about how this situation unfolded.

Two and a half decades later, I was a very different person. Not only had I learned much more about medical ethics during that time, but I had actually given professional presentations on the subject. I had come to understand that discontinuing a life-prolonging intervention was no different – from a legal perspective – than not starting it in the first place, but that – from an emotional standpoint – it *felt* different. I had been a hospice social worker longer than the vast majority of hospice social workers, and was now a go-to person not only for my social work colleagues but often for management-level staff who wanted a social work perspective. So I had found my voice when it came to challenging ethical situations. And Sandy certainly posed one.

Sandy was in her late 50s, and had a degenerative neurological disease. She had been diagnosed quite a few years ago, but over the past two years, her illness had progressed to the point that she needed to enter a nursing home for care. Initially, she had been able to get around in a power wheelchair, which enabled her to attend activities, socialize, and generally participate in the life of the facility. But now she was bedbound, unable to use any of her limbs; to summon assistance, she nudged a large call button with one elbow. Her world had shrunk to the few square feet occupied by her electric hospital bed. This would have been difficult for anyone, but it was singularly difficult for Sandy, who was an exceptionally bright and verbal woman, trapped in a nonfunctional body. Her thinking and her speech were unimpaired, so she could speak eloquently about her experiences and her feelings. Her ability to swallow was very compromised, though, so she could only eat pureed foods, and feeding her even a yogurt or a dish of applesauce was a painstaking process that could take an hour or more.

Sandy and I were close in age, and very similar in temperament; we bonded instantly. She told me she was *done*. She had given the matter extensive thought – what else did she have to do? – and she absolutely did not want to go on living like this. She was not remotely depressed, and she certainly was not suicidal; she simply did not want to wait around until she either choked to death or succumbed to an infection. She had been a sharp and in-charge person all her life, but now the disease had relentlessly stripped her of every possible control. She could not make a phone call, feed herself, or scratch her own itches, and she had to lie in her own urine and feces until someone responded to her call button and came to clean her up. The only thing that she could now control was the timing and circumstances of her own death. She was ready, she told me firmly, to "pull the plug".

Many people use this phrase, "pull the plug", and it breaks my heart when I hear it, because in most cases, there is no plug to pull. Sandy was not being kept alive by any machines, so there was nothing that we could discontinue to allow her to die naturally. We had a long hard talk, and I told her that in the state of Illinois, no physician could legally write her a prescription that she could take to end her life. This was a bit of a shock for Sandy, and she asked me what her options were. (NOTE: This is a conversation I *never* would have dared to have in the earlier years of my career, but I had since become a staunch advocate for the right of terminally ill people to decide for themselves when life was no longer worth living.) Since Sandy had no physical capability to act on her own behalf, the only thing she could do to hasten her death was to stop eating and drinking. Sandy considered this, and said she wanted to do this. However, it was not quite that simple....

First of all, Sandy was residing in a nursing facility governed by rules and regulations, one of which was that the residents all had to be provided a diet that met their particular nutritional requirements. Second, nursing homes and hospices are staffed by individual human beings who might not be comfortable with her decision and might try to dissuade her. Third, Sandy had family – an elderly mother and several siblings – who also had feelings on the matter.

Back at the office, I discussed the situation with my supervisor, and we called an internal ethics committee meeting. A lot of people who were not directly involved with Sandy's case showed up, because the subject matter was challenging and intriguing to us all. A few people (not on the committee) were very uncomfortable with Sandy's choice, and the nurse assigned to her opted to recuse herself – just as I had done with Mrs. Thorwald 25 years earlier. But the committee concluded that an alert, oriented, highly intelligent woman had the legal and moral right to refuse to eat or drink, and that there was no ethical reason not to allow this. To my amazement, the strongest voice of support came from one of the hospice's upper management staff, who said she wanted to come with me to meet Sandy.

A day or two later, we made this visit together, and then went together to talk with the nursing home's administrator, to see how he felt about this. God must have been smiling on us that day, because the nursing home administrator told us that he had previously worked for a hospice in another state, and he 100% understood where we (and Sandy) were coming from. That said, he had concerns about allowing this to transpire in his facility, because if word were to get out, they might end up with protestors picketing in the parking lot; he also was worried that some of the staff might not be supportive of Sandy's choice. So the decision was made to move Sandy to our inpatient unit for her end of life. This could not be implemented immediately, for a variety of reasons, and the events of the next few days affirmed our collective concerns: several of the nurses and nursing aides who worked in the nursing home got wind of Sandy's plans and started trying to talk her out of it.

It has been said that human beings can live three weeks without food, three days without water, and three minutes without oxygen. I don't know that this is precisely accurate, but it highlights an important point: ceasing to eat and drink is most effective when done strictly. Our understanding, when Sandy was moved to our hospice inpatient unit (IPU), was that she would refuse all food and drink, and this would probably result in her death within a week or two. But at the same time, hospice is all about keeping people comfortable, and the thing that caused Sandy the most discomfort was a dry mouth, so she often requested ice chips. It was explained to her that sucking on ice chips would prolong the process, but of course nobody was willing to deny them to her. Family dynamics also played a role: Sandy's mother and two sisters were sad but supportive of Sandy's wishes, but the other siblings could not agree with the plan. Mom and the two sisters gave Sandy ice chips when she wanted them, but the other sibs frequently tried to persuade Sandy to eat various treat foods that they had brought on their visits, which only served to cause Sandy emotional distress. I (along with the other IPU staff) spent a great deal of time listening and providing support to the family members, educating them about the dying process, and affirming that – like it or not – Sandy had the undisputable legal right to make this decision for herself. Sandy never wavered in her determination to avoid all food, but because she did suck ice chips, it ultimately was several weeks before she died. There is little to feel good about when a brilliant and talented woman dies prematurely from a terrible disease, but we who had the privilege of working with her felt blessed to have known her, and honored to have been able to help her achieve her end-of-life goal.

PART III
The Hard Stuff

17
Elder Abuse

At first blush, it might seem that elder abuse and hospice are incompatible: why would you take care of someone at home if you didn't like that person or want to take care of them? But – like most things in life – it is not that simple. Sometimes the caregiver starts out with the best of intentions, but over time, the stress of caregiving and isolation breaks her down and brings out the worst in her. Sometimes the patient is a parent who was abusive to the child, and that now-adult child has that complex love-hate relationship with him that is frequently seen in adult children of abusive parents. Sometimes the caregiving arrangement is born out of financial necessity, not love; the patient's Social Security or disability check is vital for the family's survival. The abuser is usually ashamed of his actions, so makes every effort to conceal them from the hospice team. So all team members are called upon to be keen observers of the patient and the household, and to be watchful for any indicators of possible abuse or exploitation.

Mrs. Grand was living in her own home when we first met her. Her so-called caregiver was her adult daughter, Lila, a middle-aged woman with substance abuse issues. Lila's alcoholic boyfriend lived in the house with her. When she was not intoxicated, Lila took care of household tasks such as cleaning, cooking, and shopping, which was why Mrs. Grand allowed her to live there. But, Mrs. Grand told me, Lila had made it clear that she had no intentions of providing any hands-on care when that time came. The relationship between the two women was clearly not particularly warm and fuzzy, and Mrs.

Grand had a cancer diagnosis, so she and I began discussing the option of her moving into a nursing home where she could get the physical care she was going to need. She was amenable to this, and I began searching for an appropriate facility. Because Mrs. Grand had no money other than her Social Security check, I needed to find her a nursing home that would accept her as Medicaid-pending, without a security deposit. The usual protocol in that situation is that the patient is admitted to the facility, the nursing home staff assists with the Medicaid application, and when benefits are eventually approved, they are retroactive to the date of admission. In the interim, the patient signs over whatever income she has (Social Security check, pension check, or whatever) to the nursing home, so that it receives at least partial payment while the Medicaid application is being processed. The success of this protocol is dependent on there being a family member who can work cooperatively with the facility to get them the bank statements and other financial information that is needed to apply for Medicaid.

Lila was not such a family member. While she was happy to see her mother go into a nursing home, apparently she did not initially comprehend that her mother's monthly check was leaving with her. Once she realized this, she began doing everything possible to stall the Medicaid application. When she was asked to bring in her mother's bank statements, she said she would be happy to, but she was sick at the moment and it would have to wait until she felt better. There followed a succession of thin excuses for her continuing failure to cooperate. I was caught in the middle: the nursing home's social worker complained to me that Lila was not bringing in the requested paperwork, and Lila complained to me that she was being hounded by the nursing home. As weeks became months, it became obvious to everyone that Lila had no intention of cooperating, and why. At this point, the nursing home social worker and I decided that this needed to be reported to the appropriate authorities as a case of financial exploitation; she made the necessary phone call, and I confronted Lila (by phone) to tell her that her behavior was both unacceptable and illegal, and that she had been reported.

And the next day, Mrs. Grand disappeared! According to the facility social worker, there was some other friend or relative who had come in from a neighboring state periodically to visit Mrs. Grand. On this morning, the visitor asked if she might take Mrs. Grand out for a little drive because it was a beautiful day. Off they went, and Mrs. Grand never came back. You couldn't call it a kidnapping: Mrs. Grand was a competent adult who had gone very willingly with her companion. And Mrs. Grand herself was not a criminal; the issue was with her daughter, not her. All the evidence suggested that Mrs. Grand was now in another state, so there was nothing further that I could do. The nursing home social worker did whatever our state required her to do in such a situation – I don't know what that consisted of. But the questions remained. Was this a benevolent visitor trying to remove her from the clutches of her grasping daughter? Perhaps, but the timing suggests otherwise. Was this a predatory visitor working in cahoots with Lila? We will never know. Neither the nursing home nor our hospice team ever heard another word about Mrs. Grand.

Mr. Haley lived in a city apartment. The building was a two-flat: he had the downstairs apartment, and his son and daughter-in-law lived in the upstairs unit. Mr. Haley had Parkinson's Disease: his thinking processes were intact, but his body was failing. He got around, minimally, using a walker. His daughter-in-law came downstairs at regular intervals throughout the day to provide the care that he needed, while the son went to work. Like virtually all hospice patients, over time

Mr. Haley declined, and he spent more and more time in bed. He could no longer get to the bathroom on his own, so he urinated into a urinal that he kept at bedside, and was diapered for bowel movements.

I don't know what transpired between the son and his wife, but at some point she left. Was she tired of caring for her father-in-law? Was she being abused or unappreciated by her husband? I have no idea. But one day the son made passing mention to the hospice nurse that his wife had gone, and that he was now the caregiver. This was a less-than-optimal arrangement from the get-go, as the son still had to work, so Mr. Haley was left alone for 8 to 10 hours a day. The son went downstairs first thing in the morning to change his father's diaper and give him some breakfast. He left some food and drink at bedside for Mr. Haley's lunch, and then would attend to him again in the evening when he got home. Technically his basic needs were being met, but Mr. Haley now looked forward to the hospice team's visits more than ever because we could bring him snacks, and keep him company.

One afternoon, the nurse summoned me urgently to Mr. Haley's apartment. In examining him, she had observed a massive purple bruise on his abdomen. When questioned, Mr. Haley reluctantly acknowledged that it was inflicted by his son, who had been trying to change the diaper in the morning. Normally Mr. Haley would stand up and lean heavily on his walker while his son removed the diaper, cleaned his bottom, and put on a fresh diaper. That morning, for whatever reason, Mr. Haley had been unable to stand up; he felt weak, and his knees kept buckling. The son got more and more exasperated, berating Mr. Haley for making him (the son) late for work, and finally punched Mr. Haley in the stomach. I raced over there; this had to be addressed before the son got home from work in a few more hours. Mr. Haley was amenable to being transported to our inpatient unit for safety reasons, pending making other arrangements, so the nurse got those wheels in motion while I called the elder abuse authorities and made a full report.

I fully expected that, given the unmistakable evidence of the assault, and Mr. Haley's forthcomingness about what had happened, that the son would go to jail, and that Mr. Haley would be moved into a nursing home. So I was quite surprised at what I heard when I visited him, two days later. He told me that the elder abuse investigator had come to see him at the IPU, and he had corroborated the story that I had related to her agency, but he had told her he was not willing to press charges against his son. Furthermore, he had decided he did not want to be in a nursing home, and that he wanted to return to his apartment, despite understanding that the abuse could easily recur. In our state, a mentally-competent older adult has the right to refuse elder abuse services, and they could not proceed with charges against the son without his cooperation. He *was* amenable to the agency following up with his son to provide support and/or resources, and ultimately some state-subsidized caregiver services were put into place for a few hours per day. Because the son was at work during the hours that the hospice team members made their routine visits, I was never able to follow up personally with the son, but there did not appear to be any further incidents of physical abuse.

And then there were the Pikes. Buck Pike was a man of 70, admitted to our hospice with a diagnosis of lung cancer. He and his wife Luann lived out in an unincorporated area of one of the counties I worked in – an area that seemed to be flypaper for the highly dysfunctional. Drunk and/or intoxicated driving accidents, and bar brawls were reported frequently in the local newspaper. The houses were run-down, and yards were usually occupied with broken-down vehicles and other mechanical works-in-progress. The Pike homestead was no exception. The old house looked like it was standing only due to sheer willpower, and a wheel-less car carcass sat on cement blocks alongside it.

My initial assessment visit was unusual, to say the least. Normally when I ring a doorbell, someone comes to the door to open it. In this case, a woman's voice called out, "Come in," so I gingerly let myself inside, unsure what to expect. The house's interior was on par with the exterior – stained and ragged wall-to-wall carpeting more or less covered the floor. The walls were dirty, and in one place, there was a big hole in the old plaster, as if someone had either punched it or crashed into it. I still saw no one, so I called out, "Hello! Where are you?" I followed the voice that responded, which led me to the master bedroom.

Yikes. A filthy double-bed mattress lay directly on the worn-out bare wood floor. Whatever bedding had once been on it had been tossed aside. Buck Pike lay, fully clothed on the mattress, surrounded by stains of various ages and colors. He had the large-boned frame of a man who had spent decades doing physical labor, though he now needed suspenders to hold up his pants which he was shrinking out of. Next to him lay his wife Luann. She was wearing only a t-shirt and underpants, and was curled up on her side next to him on the bed, one arm flung over his chest. When she saw me, she giggled inappropriately, and said in a slurred voice, "Hi – I'm Luann. He's Buck." Unsure how to respond to this whole situation, I smiled at her as I remarked, "Yeah, I kinda figured that."

Luann was quite obviously drunk (at noon), and as I was to learn, this was baseline for her. Although I never actually saw her with a drink in her hand, Buck later confirmed that she had been an alcoholic for many years. He expressed no concern for himself or his future care needs. He had been the one taking care of his wife for a long time, and now that he was terminally ill, he was not sure how she was going to manage once he was gone. They had brought a total of eight now-adult children into the world. He did not make clear to me who and where they all were, but he did not appear to have any expectation that any of them represented the solution to any problem. I would quickly find out why.

On one of my next visits, I met their son Scott, who had dropped by to see his parents. He was, I believe, their youngest, and looked to be no more than thirty years old. In those early days of my career, I still believed that most family members would want to talk about their feelings of grief and loss if given the opportunity, so I attempted to engage Scott in some conversation about the situation. It was 10 AM and Scott had a beer in his hand, which (in retrospect) should have been my first clue. He was also smoking a cigarette. As we chatted, he asked me to grab him the ashtray that was on a nearby table. His request struck me as odd, since he appeared able-bodied, and the ashtray was as close to him as it was to me, but I complied. As I leaned over to reach the ashtray, Scott said, "You have a nice ass." I was stunned, and sat back down (on my nice ass) quickly. By the grace of God, this was a joint visit with our hospice nurse Roxie, a solid and no-nonsense gal who I'm sure could have taken Scott in a fight. She was near enough to overhear his remark, and came to my rescue, telling Scott in no uncertain terms that this was unacceptable behavior and that he needed to do any future visiting at times when none of the hospice team members were on the premises.

Soon thereafter, we met Rhonda, one of the Pikes' daughters. She had come in from some other state, ostensibly to take care of her parents. She took care of them alright: she took care of cleaning out their savings account, I later learned, and then bailed back to wherever she had come from. I learned this from Dana, the daughter who rode in on her white horse (figuratively speaking) to chase the predatory Rhonda away, only to pick up right where Rhonda had left off. In this manner, the hospice team eventually met the majority of the Pikes' offspring, each of whom left the parents in some manner worse off than before. Buck seemed resigned to all of this, and did not want to pursue any legal action against any of the children. Luann stayed drunk.

As Buck declined, he had no energy to do anything except sit on the couch and watch TV. Once he had walked from his bed to the couch, he had no more energy left for any other activities. Luann generally sat with him. As impaired as she usually appeared, she was apparently able to cook at least simple meals to keep them both alive. But she was not well either. She complained of frequent severe stomach aches, which did not surprise any of the hospice team, as she ate very little and seemed to be getting most of her daily calories from alcohol. Roxie the nurse encouraged Luann to see a doctor about these stomach pains, but of course Luann did not go.

Then one morning, my team manager informed me that Luann had died the evening before. *What??!* He was not sure what had transpired, but we agreed that I needed to go to the home right away to talk with Buck. As usual, Buck sat on his sagging couch, but today he looked as if all the air had been let out of him. The story that emerged was horrifying. They were sitting watching TV the evening before – Buck on the couch, and Luann in a nearby chair -- when Luann was suddenly gripped by stomach pain. The pain seemed even worse than it normally was, and she gasped and clutched at her chest. Before he could ask her what was wrong, she gasped again, her eyes rolled back in her head, and she toppled sideways off the chair onto the floor. Buck was physically unable to get up from the couch and go to her, so he sat there helplessly while she died in front of him. With 20/20 hindsight, the stomach pain Luann had been complaining of was probably actually heart-related, but we will never know.

Another son, Don, showed up later that evening, and it was he who called 911, and our office. From that point on, a shadowy cadre of people (friends? neighbors? former coworkers?) came and went, to see to it that at least Buck's most basic needs were met. Buck was alone most of the time, and very vague with us about who was actually doing what, but he seemed content and did not want to make any changes such as moving into a nursing home. With Luann gone, he had no more reason to hang on, and he died in his home just a few weeks after she did.

18
The Hoarder

I was covering for a vacationing coworker, when I was asked to do an initial assessment on Mr. Willits. My computer informed me that he was an elderly man with a bad heart. He and his wife lived in a working-class suburb with which I was not very familiar, but my GPS got me there. Their wood-frame house was small and old, like all the other houses on that block. The front yard looked a bit neglected, but not vastly different than the neighbors'. Mrs. Willits, walking slowly with a cane, opened the door when I rang the bell.

No lights were on inside the house, and it took my eyes a moment to adjust to the gloom. But as soon as I glanced around, I could see that this was a hoarder house. The tiny front room contained a small, tired sofa and an overstuffed reclining armchair. An unlit floor lamp cowered in the corner. Everywhere else, there were piles and piles of magazines and newspapers. A 3-foot tall heap of newspapers served as an end table next to the couch, providing a resting place for Mrs. Willits' cigarette pack and ashtray. Every space that was not occupied by paper was filled with plastic storage boxes, stacked one atop another. There was just enough room between the piles for a person to walk, which is how the couple was able to get around in the house. I mentally connected the dots between all those papers, and Mrs. Willits' smoking, and realized the whole place was a terrible fire trap if she should drop an ember, or fall asleep with a cigarette in hand. I also worried about Mrs. Willits' impaired walking ability: if she were to fall, it would be difficult for EMS even to find her, let alone extricate her.

Mr. Willits was lying on the bed in what used to be the couple's bedroom. That room also was crammed with storage boxes and miscellanea, creating the effect of a contiguous surface at the height of the mattress. Mrs. Willits explained to me that it was too difficult for them to share a bed, for various reasons, so she had decamped to the sofa a long time ago. He was, at this point in his illness, too weak and sick to talk with me, and the nurse had said that he really needed to be in a hospital bed, in order to elevate his upper body so that he could breathe more easily. He also needed to be on oxygen. The obvious problem, however, was that there was no possible place to put these items.

It is challenging, in situations like this, to thoroughly explore the situation, and consider options, without coming across as judgmental. Hoarding is not something I'd consider an area of expertise for me, but I know that hoarders generally keep excessive amounts of stuff for a variety of emotional reasons that have nothing to do with the inherent value of the items. Fortunately in this instance it was not so severe that the house was overrun with vermin or rotting garbage, but it was still unsafe. Figuring out why Mrs. Willits had begun hoarding, or how to clear out the whole house, was far beyond my purview. But we needed to resolve the practical issue of how we could get the medical equipment that Mr. Willits required into the home.

Since Mrs. Willits did want our hospice to be able to come in and provide services to her husband, she was quite receptive to discussing the impediments with me. It was obvious that neither she nor her husband was capable of moving anything around, and their only child was a son in another state who had entirely disconnected himself from his parents many years earlier. It was also obvious that they had no money to pay for any help, and they were quite socially isolated: there were no neighbors or church friends who might volunteer to do some cleaning up.

I asked her point-blank if I could just start throwing out some of those magazines and newspapers, but she said no, without explanation. The piles were already tall enough that they could not be consolidated in order to clear out some space. I made a couple more suggestions about how to re-arrange or dispose of what (to me) seemed like worthless crap, but she was resistant to these ideas. I decided that I shouldn't be working harder at solving the problem than she was, so I turned it back over to her: "Why don't *you* tell me what I could move or get rid of, so that we can get that hospital bed and an oxygen concentrator in here?" To my surprise, she said she was willing to dispatch the armchair. She explained to me that this had been her husband's chair, and since he could no longer walk to the living room to sit in it, it didn't need to be there anymore.

The chair was ratty enough that most people would have thrown it out, but I knew better than to assume this. When I asked her what should be done with the chair, she said she would like it moved into the garage. This is why I always wear slacks and comfortable shoes to work – you just never know what the day may bring…. There was nobody else around to ask, so I wrestled the armchair out the front door, dragged it across the lawn and the driveway, and deposited it in the garage (which actually wasn't nearly as cluttered as the house).

Mrs. Willits felt that the problem was now solved, but I pointed out to her that the footprint of the chair wasn't nearly the size of a hospital bed. To keep the conversation objective, I called the DME (durable medical equipment) company, and asked them for precise dimensions of both the hospital bed and the oxygen concentrator. Quite randomly, I happened to have a yardstick in the trunk of my car, so I brought it in to show her precisely how big an area was required. More negotiations ensued, and eventually Mrs. Willits was willing to let me relocate several piles of magazines and newspapers to the garage – just enough to accommodate the DME. Without further ado, I called the DME company back and asked them to deliver the bed and oxygen ASAP, before Mrs. Willits could change her mind or fill up the empty space again.

By this time, I had been at the home for nearly three hours, and was both physically and emotionally exhausted. I told Mrs. Willits that I was very pleased to have met her, and that I hoped I had been of some assistance. I tried not to appear too overjoyed as I explained to her that I was only covering for her regularly-assigned social worker, so would probably not be seeing her again.

19
The Old Soldier

I was asked to go to the nursing home to provide support to Mr. Albrecht's family. He was in his late seventies, and dying imminently. When I arrived, the only family member present was his tearful middle-aged daughter Rose. Mr. Albrecht himself lay in his hospital bed, unresponsive but seemingly comfortable. I pulled up a chair, and encouraged Rose to reminisce about her father. There is substantial evidence that even at this stage of the dying process, people can still hear and understand, even if they cannot speak, so I regularly urged family members at the bedside to share their positive recollections.

Rose sniffled as she told me that he had been a wonderful father to her, and husband to her mother. She told me how he read stories to her at bedtime when she was very small, and what a good cook he was. She had had an idyllic childhood until World War Two came along, and he went off to be a soldier. He was taken captive, and held as a prisoner of war for several years, a period of separation and deprivation that was extremely hard on his wife and young child. He was fortunate to survive this terrible internment, and eventually returned home, where her fond relationship with him resumed where it had left off. He never talked about his wartime experiences, but she was proud that he had worn a uniform and served his country.

Mr. Albrecht began to breathe a bit more irregularly, and I took a moment to explain to Rose that this was a sign that his body was shutting down and death was near. She began to cry, and to my surprise, proceeded to crawl into the hospital bed next to her father, and snuggle against him like a little girl. Her childlike grief tugged at my own heartstrings, and I could see what this noble old soldier meant to her.

After a while, she got back out of the bed, sat back down on her chair, and we resumed talking. She seemed to want to tell me more about his painful absence from the household during her childhood, and I listened attentively, affirming how hard this must have been for her. Then she happened to mention a few important details that changed everything for me. Her early childhood had been, not in the United States, but in Germany. Her father had been interned, not in a Polish or German concentration camp, but in Russia. I realized, to my horror, that the man I was looking at in this bed was a former Nazi soldier.

I had to struggle to maintain a neutral facial expression as a surge of revulsion rose within me. My sympathy for the daughter evaporated in an instant. My own family is Jewish, and though none of my own ancestors lived in Nazi Germany, Jews from everywhere take the nightmare of the Holocaust very personally. How could a Nazi soldier have been a tender husband and a loving father?? I could not reconcile this in my own mind.

But, after some moments of internal struggle, I managed to regain some perspective and equanimity. I was not there to sit in judgment. I was there to provide support to a hurting fellow human, regardless of whether or not I could relate to her specific circumstances. Grief is grief, in every country and in every language. Sometimes we are called upon to tolerate ambiguity, and to let the unanswerable questions go unanswered.

20
Death (and its Aftermath)
Without Dignity

In hospice we often speak of "death with dignity" as a goal for our patients. But some deaths are utterly devoid of dignity, through no fault of our own.

Somewhere during my first few months as a hospice social worker, I was asked to go see a patient, Mr. Wilson, who lived in a very poor neighborhood. His situation was extreme even by the standards of poverty, however. He was a relatively young Black man, dying of lung cancer. He was living – if you could call it that – in the basement of a condemned house. The windows were boarded up, but I was told which sheet of plywood I needed to move in order to lower myself onto the stepladder inside, and then climb down it to where my patient was lying on a filthy mattress on the concrete floor. There were no utilities or running water in the building. A bucket nearby was his toilet. I asked how he was eating, and he said that a friend came by daily with a sack of food from McDonald's. I asked him if he wanted to be moved to some place where he could receive care, and he was quite adamant that he wanted to stay where he was. This was to be the only time I saw him, as he died not long afterwards. I wish I had been able to learn more of his story. And I wish I had been able to somehow make the end of his life better.

Another young Black patient in a very poor neighborhood – this time, a 22-year-old woman named Latisha who died of cancer the day after her admission to hospice. The decrepit wooden house had an illegal second-floor room addition which had been her bedroom. An impossibly narrow and angled staircase had been shoe-horned into the structure to access that room. The hospice nurse and I attended her death. Because Latisha had just been admitted to hospice, and because her family had been in denial and disbelief about her condition, there were no funeral plans. I sat with her weeping mother and together we thumbed through the Yellow Pages phonebook to decide whom to call. Eventually the mother picked out a funeral home, and called them. A short time later, Mr. Funeral Director arrived, by himself, wheeling his gurney. He struck me as a pompous man: although he was there to pick up a dead body, he was wearing a three-piece suit made from a shiny jacquard fabric, and equally shiny dress shoes. He was also a rather rotund man, and the nurse and I exchanged glances as we both realized there was no way he was going to be able maneuver either himself or his cart, singlehandedly, up and down those stairs; a brief conversation between him and the nurse confirmed this. It was clear that he expected *us* to bring Latisha down the awkward staircase, and since his cart would not fit, we were going to have to improvise. Up at the top of the stairs, we saw Latisha lying on her bed, and we discussed in whispers what to do. We could not just carry her like a sack of potatoes, so the nurse suggested that we wrap her, burrito-style, in the bedsheet, and then each of us would grab one end of it. In this manner, we staggered down the narrow stairs, our awkward bundle swaying between us, and multiple family members looking on while we tried not to let her bump against the wall or the railing that pressed in on us. We laid her carefully on the gurney, whereupon Mr. Funeral Director promptly zipped up the body bag in front of the whole family. The mother and grandmother promptly began to wail and keen loudly, and the grandmother threw her large body across Latisha's slender frame, sobbing. The nurse and I did our best to provide support, and I made a mental note never to use that particular funeral home again.

Mr. Eisen was an elderly Jewish man with a very bad heart. He lived in a small, cramped townhouse with his adult son, who provided most of his care; an adult daughter lived nearby and visited daily, bringing favorite foods. The layout of the townhouse was unusual: the entire living space was over the garage, so the entry stairway was steep and narrow, and delivered visitors right into the living room. Eventually Mr. Eisen died, the funeral home was called, and the two men arrived with their cart. The more slender and athletic of the two held the bottom, while the man at the upper end of it was a large, stocky fellow. In order to hold onto his end of the gurney, he had to walk backwards up the stairs. When the heftier man reached the top of the stairs, he continued walking backwards so that they could bring the full length of the cart into the room. Neither of these gentlemen had much situational awareness, and both of them failed to notice that there was a glass-topped coffee table directly in their path. Before anyone could intervene, the larger man had backed right into it, lost his balance, and crashed heavily on his *tuchus* through the thick glass. Fortunately he was unharmed (except, perhaps, for wounded pride), but we were all so shocked that for a moment, nobody moved or said a word. As I was the closest to him, I extended my hand and helped him stand up. He dusted himself off and straightened his rumpled suit. Given the circumstances, I thought that he would apologize to the family for his clumsiness, but he did not. The rest of the removal proceeded without incident, but his carelessness – and failure to apologize – left an extra measure of gloom after their departure.

Please do not take the foregoing stories as indications of any animosity on my part towards funeral directors. On the contrary, hospice staff and funeral directors work very closely together, and over the years I forged strong working relationships with many of them (and in one instance, a personal friendship as well). But just as there are no do-overs in hospice, there are no do-overs with funeral directors either, and it saddens me when a family's last moments with their loved one are tainted by pomposity or insensitivity.

21
It Sucks When It's a Little Kid

I did not expect, when I began my hospice work, that I would be working with children. Of course I knew, intellectually, that children sometimes die of various diseases, but I did not equate that with hospice; all the hospice patients I had heard about were middle-aged or elderly people. About three years into my career, I was handed a piece of paper with my newest case assignment. As I walked back towards my desk, I saw that the patient was a 4-year-old boy with a terminal neurodegenerative illness. My own oldest son was 4 years old, and had the same first name. My eyes began to fill. By the time I actually got to my seat, I was crying, imagining how devastated I would be were this my own child. I didn't even bother to sit down. I did an about-face, marched back to my manager's office, and told her tearfully, "I can't do this one. Fire me, shoot me, or do whatever you want to me, but I cannot get past the fact that this is a little boy the same age and same name as my oldest son." Fortunately, she was very understanding, and said she would assign him to another of the social workers. But that remained a sticking point for me, and I was never able to come to terms with working with terminally ill little kids. The hospice that I worked for the longest had a dedicated (in both senses of that word) pediatric team, so I was very grateful that I was rarely asked to involve myself with pediatric hospice.

When you are on-call, however, you have to take what you get. One night, I was called to attend the death of a pediatric patient – a little 2-year-old girl who had succumbed at last to a congenital abnormality. I told the nurse who was fielding the phone calls that I was horrified about having to go on this particular visit. She was an older, highly-experienced nurse who had done everything at least once, and she reassured me, "Don't worry – you'll be fine. I've seen this before – they look like little angels." Since I had no choice in the matter anyway, off I went to the home. The family had been well-prepared all along, so they had been expecting the baby's death; they were sad and grieving, but not hysterical. They were solid people, doing a good job of supporting one another. I went from one to another, expressing my condolences and listening to whatever they felt like sharing.

The baby was lying on a beautiful blanket on the sofa, and of course I went over to take a good hard look at her. She was a pretty little girl, and the mother had clothed her in a sweet dress and bonnet. But my nurse had lied to me: the girl did not look like a little angel -- she looked very much like a dead baby. The adorable outfit could not camouflage the pale waxy skin of death, and I winced inwardly. Eventually the funeral director arrived, wheeling in his adult-sized gurney. I cringed again, imagining how forlorn the tiny body would look, adrift on that large cart. The mother, however, who looked about as sad as any human being could possibly look, put her hand on the funeral director's arm to stop him. "I will carry her out," she informed the man. She swaddled her baby in the blanket, picked her up with all of a mother's tenderness, and slowly walked out to the funeral director's waiting SUV. All the rest of us processed out behind her, and there was nary a dry eye as she laid the little bundle down in the back of the vehicle.

I cried all the way home.

PART IV
The Funny Stuff

22
Hospice Humor

It probably seems oxymoronic to juxtapose those two words, but I assure you, scratch the surface of most hospice workers, and you will find a fairly sick sense of humor. It is a rare patient or family that ever catches a glimpse of this – and only if they have first demonstrated to us that they see some dark humor in the situation – but behind the closed doors of our offices and our cars, we let our hair down with our coworkers. In truth, it is a coping mechanism: we are dealing with death and dying on a daily basis, and horrible jokes are one way to shake off some of the heaviness.

The uninitiated might not realize how many humorous euphemisms there are for dying. "I told him not to buy any green bananas," we quip among ourselves. (No, we don't really tell our patients that.) People who are close to death are described as "on the checkout stand". The newly-dead is "ART" = Assuming Room Temperature. "Gone tits up" speaks for itself. "Pushing up daisies", "checking out the grass from underneath", "taking a dirt nap", and "worm chow" describe someone already buried.

Occasionally there are things that occur in hospice that are genuinely funny (again, at least to the staff). When I had been working in hospice for a few years, I found myself teamed up with a nurse named Dina. She was relatively new to nursing, and quite young, but she was very bright and caring, and I liked working with her. One day we went together to attend the death of our patient, Mr. Cacciatore. He and his wife were relatively-recent Italian immigrants who spoke fair-to-middling English.

His wife and their adult daughter were rather superstitious. Mr. Cacciatore had died in his bed, and the undershirt he had been wearing was rather soiled, so Dina and I decided to clean him up a bit to make him more presentable to the family. As Dina lifted his upper body and leaned him forward so that I could remove the undershirt, whatever air remained in his lungs was squeezed out by this movement, with the result that the dead Mr. Cacciatore emitted a loud groan. His wife shrieked, and the daughter started to cry. Dina did her best to explain to them that he really was dead, and that the noise was just caused by the pressure on his diaphragm, but honestly, it took every bit of our self-control not to burst out laughing.

When you inhabit the medical world, it is easy to forget that many people outside of that bubble are not at all savvy about how the human body works, or fails to. I was in the office one day when a call was put through to one of the hospice nurses. Because her hands were occupied with some task, she put the call on speaker, so I was able to hear both sides of the conversation. The daughter of one of her patients said, "I think Momma is dead." The nurse noted the daughter's choice of words, and asked why she thought that. The daughter replied, "Because she keeps pushing the oxygen thing out of her nose." Several of us who were within earshot had to run out of the room so that our guffaws would not be heard over the phone.

And then there was Mr. Benson. His wife was our patient for several months before dying of her cardiac condition, so I got to know both of them pretty well. She was a force to be reckoned with, and there was a very clear division of labor between the two of them. The kitchen and the checkbook were two areas where Mrs. Benson had ruled with an iron fist throughout their long marriage, which made for a difficult transition as she declined. But Mr. Benson gradually learned to cook at least enough to sustain himself, and he assumed the paying of their bills when she was no longer able to do so.

After Mrs. Benson died, I did not expect to see her husband again. But one day -- some months later -- I was walking in the neighborhood where they had lived and, to my surprise, saw Mr. Benson headed up the sidewalk, smiling at me as he approached. We chatted for a bit, and he told me that he was doing pretty well. Then he chuckled, and proceeded to tell me this story:

A few weeks after his wife's death, Mr. Benson decided he could not live indefinitely on microwaved TV dinners and scrambled eggs, and concluded that he needed to expand his culinary repertoire. He decided to broil some hamburgers. Vaguely recalling that ovens are supposed to be preheated, he turned it on and left the kitchen. When he returned, he was greeted with the smell of something burning, and smoke emanating from the oven, though he had not yet put the burgers in. He yanked open the broiler, and found a burning brown paper bag, which he hastily tossed into the sink. He had belatedly discovered his late wife's hiding place for cash, and had just partially incinerated several thousand dollars!

23

Jailbreak at Money Meadows

"Calling Dr. White for Mrs. Astor! Calling Dr. White for Mrs. Astor!" These words were echoing through the overhead paging system at Money Meadows when I walked in to visit my patients there. No, it was not really called Money Meadows, but since it was far and away the most posh and most expensive nursing home in the area, it might as well have been. I had been seeing hospice patients there for many years, and I knew the code. There was no Dr. White on staff – paging "Dr. White" was the staff's way to communicate that their resident Mrs. Astor had, as they say in nursing home jargon, "eloped". In other words, they couldn't find her.

Bernice Astor was not one of my hospice patients, but I knew who she was. She was an elderly lady in the middle stages of dementia, and she was quite a character. Mrs. Astor had married money – several times – and she was very fond of the male of our species. Having outlived Wealthy Husband #3, she had no spouse coming to visit her, so she had to make do with whomever was available on the unit where she resided. There was a dapper older fellow who was a retired physician, and was always impeccably dressed in his wheelchair, including one or another of his colorful bowties. While the other male residents were addressed as Mr. So-and-So by the respectful staff, the retired physician was of course addressed as Dr. Bloomfield. Mrs. Astor might not have been able to remember how to brush her teeth, how to put her dress on right-side out, or who her daughter was, but she evidently remembered that the title "Doctor" generally equated to money. Accordingly, she attached herself to Dr. Bloomfield, often sitting next to him at activities, and sometimes holding his hand. This went on for some time, until the day that *Mrs.* Bloomfield happened to arrive and found Mrs. Astor sitting on the good doctor's lap in his wheelchair. The director of nursing had a discreet but immediate chat with Mrs. Astor's daughter, urging her strongly to hire a private-duty caregiver to keep Mrs. Astor productively occupied, and off of Dr. Bloomfield.

The private-duty caregiver had indeed been hired, but she was only part-time and had already left for the day. Most of the Money Meadows residents, including Mrs. Astor, napped after lunch, but today she was nowhere to be found. Although Mrs. Astor had dementia, she was a very attractive older woman who liked to be dressed nicely. She always carried a purse, though it contained nothing but tissues. Her social graces were intact, and she said a cheerful hello to everyone she encountered. She looked more like a visitor than a resident, so the staff were justifiably concerned that she might have walked right out the front door when the receptionist had her back turned, and that she would not be immediately recognizable out on the street as a wayward resident. The director of nursing had her coat on already, and told me she was going to walk up and down the busy street to see if she saw Mrs. Astor heading to one of the nearby restaurants.

I went about my business while other staff continued searching room to room. By the time I finished visiting my various hospice patients, Mrs. Astor had been found, and one of the nurses was able to tell me the happy ending to this story. Evidently Mrs. Astor had indeed been tired and wanted to take a nap, but her desire to crawl into bed did not happen to coincide with the aide's availability to tuck her in. Mrs. Astor did not remember how to find her room, so wandered around until she saw a nametag that read "Bernice" on one of the doors. This room actually belonged to another resident with that same first name, who was attending an activity. Mrs. Astor climbed into the other Bernice's bed and snuggled up under the covers, so when staff made their rounds, they assumed that the person in the bed was the rightful occupant of that room.

You know what they say about "never assume"....

24
You Two Need to Talk

Spouses – especially elderly ones – are often very protective of one another. So I was not surprised when I paid my initial visit to Mr. Klein, and Mrs. Klein immediately drew me into the kitchen to speak privately with me. She told me that her husband was in their bedroom, lying down, but she wanted to tell me something important before I could meet with him. "He has cancer," she began. "He knows that, but he doesn't know that he's dying. Promise me you won't tell him."

I replied to this as I always did to such requests – assuring her that I would not bring it up, but that I *would* answer his questions honestly if he asked. In my experience, I explained to her, people don't ask if they don't want to know; conversely, if someone does ask, it is unconscionable to lie to them, even though the news may be hard to hear. Most people have things that they would want to do or say if they knew that their time was very limited. Once the initial shock has worn off and the tears dry, they want to update their Will, tell close family members how much they love them, and/or show their spouse where the important papers are. So hospice professionals feel strongly that patients have the right to get a truthful answer if they are asking questions about their disease or prognosis.

Mrs. Klein accepted my response, introduced me to her husband, and left the room. As soon as she was out of earshot, Mr. Klein hissed to me, "Close the door. I need to tell you something important." He proceeded to tell me, "I have cancer. My wife knows that, but she doesn't know that I'm going to die. I don't want you to tell her."

I smiled as I affirmed that he was obviously a loving husband who cared deeply about his wife's wellbeing. But I had to tell him that she had just spoken precisely the same words to me about him. He seemed quite surprised.

He and I conversed for a few minutes, and then I said I was going to get his wife. I ushered Mrs. Klein into the bedroom, then told them, "I'll come back later this week to follow up with you, but right now, you two need to talk."

25
The Last Hurrah

I do not know the physiological explanation for this, but it is often observed that the dying person has a final burst of alertness and energy in the 24-48 hours prior to death. Over the years, I saw this many times, but I will never forget my first encounter with this phenomenon.

Mr. DeVroom was a 93-year-old widowed nursing home resident. He was dying of cancer, and when he was admitted to our hospice, he was only minimally responsive. I knew him only as a wizened little man in a hospital bed. His daughter, Angela, gave me some background information, and said that she just wanted her father to be comfortable, which he appeared to be. A couple of weeks after he was admitted, Mr. DeVroom died over a weekend. On Monday, I called Angela to offer my condolences, and to hear what she might wish to share about the particulars of his death. On Saturday afternoon, she told me, she had gone to visit her father, expecting to find him sleeping as he usually was. But to her surprise, he was sitting up in bed, eyes wide open and bright, lustily singing a folk song in the language of his native country. He did not seem to recognize her as his daughter, but when she approached the bedside and asked if she could do anything for him, he barked, "Yes – get me a beer and a woman!" I'm sure I gasped, and I asked Angela, "So ... what did you do?" She chuckled sheepishly and replied, "Well, I got him the beer...." He drank the beer, then drifted off to sleep. On Sunday, he never woke up.

PART V
The Power of the Spirit

26

Sometimes the Chaplain is a Social Worker

Being a social worker and being a spiritual human are not mutually exclusive. In fact, in my experience, the vast majority of my coworkers – whatever their discipline – were people of profound faith, and felt that their hospice work had a deeply spiritual significance. For me, one of the reasons I stayed in this work for so long was my strong sense of *calling*: my hospice work was a ministry, not merely a job.

I make a habit of praying before I start my day, asking that God will lead me to the people who need me, and that I will recognize and rise to those occasions when they occur. Whether during my workday or on my own time, I call these "God-moments", and I have found that if I open myself to these opportunities, they will present themselves. One time, when my husband and I were on vacation together, I found myself in the motel's laundry room with another guest. She had forgotten her laundry in the only dryer, and showed up, full of apologies, just as I was debating whether to dump her clothes out on the folding table. She explained that she was very preoccupied because her mother was about to undergo serious surgery at the nearby hospital. I immediately asked if she would like me to pray with her for her mother, and she was startled but appreciative. Incredibly, we both ended up in the same laundry room at the same time a couple of days later, and she gratefully reported that her mother had come through the surgery remarkably well.

Being on-call was, for me, the hands-down most stressful aspect of hospice work. To be sure, the social worker doesn't get called nearly as frequently as the nurse, but I have just never done well with being jarred out of a sound sleep by a ringing phone, and having to rush out the door and drive to parts unknown while still only half-awake. Also, at nights and on weekends, the on-call staff need to be available to many patients and geographical areas that are not their normal responsibilities. Prayer, and inviting God to make this *His* on-call shift, not mine, helped me manage the intense anxiety I would otherwise experience.

Late one night, I received a call from one of our hospice inpatient units. The IPU nurse told me that a patient had just died, and the family was requesting a chaplain. Our hospice used a "counselor on-call" system, meaning that at any given time, either a social worker or a chaplain was available to provide support, but not both simultaneously. Most of the time, this arrangement was adequate, and saved some wear-and-tear on the chaplains and social workers by reducing the number of on-call shifts each of us had to take. But sometimes the on-call need was for something specific to one or the other of those disciplines, and that was the case here: the family wanted a chaplain to come pray with them before the patient's body was removed by the funeral director.

I explained to the nurse that I was a social worker, but also a person of faith; if the family truly needed a particular clergy (rabbi, priest, imam), I would try to find such a person in the community, but if they simply wanted prayer support, I would be happy to offer that myself. The nurse went to check with the family, and reported back to me that they would be quite content with a prayerful social worker, so I slipped my shoes on, grabbed my rolling bag, and began the 20-mile drive to the IPU.

In the darkened room, I saw the outlines of a terribly emaciated woman who looked no more than mid-forties. Clearly a cancer death. At the foot of the bed stood a somber-looking young man and woman. I introduced myself, offered condolences, and asked them to tell me a bit of their story so that I would know how best to pray for them.

The story that emerged was heartbreaking. As a very young woman, the patient had gotten pregnant, in circumstances where she knew she would be unable to care for the child. She gave the baby up for adoption, and sadly, continued in her rather self-destructive lifestyle. The baby had been adopted by a loving couple, and had grown up to be the young man who now stood before me. When he reached adulthood, he made three very important life choices: he became a Christian, he married the caring woman who now stood at his side, and he decided that he needed to find his birth mother. About a year ago, he had at last tracked her down. By this time, she had conquered her demons, and was thrilled to be reunited with the son she had given up more than twenty years earlier. Their connection had been tentative at first, but warmed rapidly as they got to know one another. Then, just as the son was rejoicing in their restored relationship, she was diagnosed with ovarian cancer that had already metastasized extensively; there was little to be done except keep her comfortable.

My eyes came perilously close to overflowing as his story unfolded, and I thanked him for sharing it so candidly. We joined hands as I thanked God for his birth mother, and prayed that in death she had found the peace that had so eluded her for most of her life. I prayed for peace, understanding, and acceptance for her son and daughter-in-law as well. They in turn thanked God for sending me, and prayed blessings for my drive home. At the end, we exchanged heartfelt hugs. I helped them select a funeral home; once that was arranged, they left because they did not want to stay to see her beleaguered body carried out.

As for me, I drove home thanking God for this opportunity, and feeling that I had received far more than I had given.

27
Visitations

It is hardwired into human nature to wonder what happens at the moment of death, and thereafter. I do not claim to have all those answers, but I can share my own observations with you. While I cannot provide scientific studies or precise numbers, I can say that a significant percentage of my hospice patients appear to have had some sort of experience of "the other side" shortly before their deaths. Many patients have told me (or one of their family members) that they were visited by a deceased loved one – usually a mother or grandmother. In some cases, the patient was asleep and experienced this in a dream, which perhaps we can chalk up to wishful thinking. But in many cases the recipient of the visit was wide awake at the time, and others who were there confirmed that the patient was conscious and otherwise lucid (although the others present could not see or hear the "visitor" themselves). Lest you dismiss this as a hallucination caused by medications, I can attest that many of the patients who had such experiences were not on any medications whatsoever. And neither was the experience conditioned by religious training, because in many cases the patient was non-religious and was quite taken aback by the visit, which represented to them an afterlife in which they did not otherwise believe. In the vast majority of situations, the patient found the visit comforting – a reassurance that their loved one would be waiting for them. Let me tell you just a couple of these many stories.

Martha resided in a nursing home, dying slowly from metastatic bone cancer. She was a deeply religious Catholic, a single woman in her early 60s. Her younger sister, Mary, came to visit (for real) at least once or twice a week, as did a couple of other family members; Martha did not have a big social circle, and her only other visitors were the members of her hospice team. Mary needed a hip replacement, and before she went into the hospital for her surgery, she told Martha that she would not be able to visit for a while because she would be going into a skilled rehabilitation facility after the operation. This was long before cellphones and laptops, and Martha did not have a landline phone in the nursing home, so no visit meant no communication. Martha calmly accepted this, and wished her well. Mary's surgery proceeded uneventfully, but a few days into her rehab, she developed a blood clot that became a pulmonary embolism and killed her, extremely unexpectedly.

Martha's niece (Mary's daughter) was beside herself with grief and apprehension: she wanted to tell Martha the news in person, but was unable to go to the nursing home for the next several days. She called me to tell me about this terrible development, and made a point of instructing me that *nobody* was to say one word to Martha about Mary's death until she (the niece) was able to break the news herself. Of course I agreed, and asked her to let me know when she had done so. A few days later, the niece called me. She had gone to the nursing home to tell Martha the sad news about Mary. To the niece's great surprise, Martha replied that she already knew. The niece's initial reaction was fury: she assumed that either another relative or I had spilled the beans after being told explicitly not to. She demanded of Martha, "Who told you??" Martha responded that Mary herself had told her: Mary had appeared in her room, informed Martha that she had died, but was in a wonderful place and was OK. When I visited with Martha the next day, she told me the same story. Martha said she was very much at peace with Mary's death, and knew now that Mary would be waiting for her.

Another patient was an elderly woman. My interactions in this case were mainly with her only child, an adult daughter whom I will call Janet. After her mother died, I called Janet to offer my condolences, and as I routinely do on these calls, I asked her to share with me her experience of what her mother's death had been like. Janet told me that she spent several hours with her mother that day, and was present at the time of death. The mother had been minimally responsive over the past 24 hours. Just before she died, Janet recounted to me, her mother suddenly opened her eyes, smiled broadly, and folded her arms to her chest as if holding something; then, just as suddenly, she closed her eyes again, and was gone. Janet thought this was odd, and did not know what to make of it.

She began calling the immediate family to inform them of the death, and soon Janet's aunt (the patient's sister) arrived on the scene. In the course of conversation, Janet told her aunt about the strange behavior she had witnessed just before her mother's final breath. The aunt blurted out, "Oh my God – she saw the baby!" Janet had no idea what her aunt was talking about. The aunt proceeded to explain. A few years before Janet was born, the mother had given birth to a child, who died in infancy. This was many years ago, and as was customary in those days, the mother was told that she should just forget about it, and that she could have other children. Nobody ever talked about the baby who had died, and Janet never knew that she had briefly had an older sibling. Janet's father was long-deceased, and the only other living relative who knew about the baby was this aunt. I found this story singularly interesting, because neither Janet nor her aunt had any expectations that this deathbed reunion might occur, and it exposed a decades-old family tragedy.

Early in my hospice career, I was not sure what to think about the reports of deceased people visiting their dying relatives. But – after hearing many such stories, and particularly, the two described above – I came to accept them at face value. I regularly use stories to make teaching points with the families I work with, and I often shared these accounts (minus the names) with them. I have come to call these visitations the "welcoming committee", and I believe that every dying person has one. For each person who is about to depart this life, somebody somewhere is waiting just for him or her on the other shore.

28
Dogs (and the Occasional Cat) Know

I've said it before, and I'll say it again now: I'm a cat person. I just naturally get along with cats and know how to read them. I would even say that I can speak their language to a degree. (My husband, who has heard me meow at other people's cats, would vouch for this.) It is a rare cat that doesn't respond well to me. Dogs, on the other hand, I don't quite get. With apologies to all the dog-lovers out there, I don't like how most dogs smell, and I don't like being slobbered on. There have been a few individual dogs that I loved dearly, and I've met a lot of adorable puppies, but I have an across-the-board affinity for felines that I just don't have for canines.

In all my years of going in and out of my patients' homes, I never had a single negative encounter with a cat. There were a few scaredy-cats that never came out from under the couch, but of all the ones who put in an appearance, none ever scratched, bit, or hissed at me. I can't say the same for dogs. I had one patient who lived in the home of his daughter, who had three medium-sized poodles. These dogs were very high-strung, and got completely hysterical each time any of the hospice staff visited, so the daughter regularly closed them up in a room when she knew we were coming to see her father. One day the daughter had to go somewhere, and forgot that I had scheduled a visit. When I arrived, the cleaning lady opened the door. She had no idea what to do with the dogs, who scrambled to the door with her. The minute I crossed the threshold, the dogs went airborne, leaping up repeatedly and barking wildly. There was a stunned moment in which both the cleaning lady and I froze, unsure what to do. In that moment, one of the poodles jumped on me, and bit my thigh. That was enough for me – I told the cleaning lady I was leaving. Fortunately, I was wearing a heavy denim jumper, so the bite did not penetrate the skin. But the pooch had bitten me hard enough that I had distinct purple tooth marks on my leg. Of course this incident had to be reported to my supervisor immediately, and she sent me directly to the occupational health office to be examined. The doctor was legally obligated to report the dog bite to the appropriate state authorities, which caused all hell to break loose: all three dogs had to be impounded and quarantined, and I was *persona non grata* in that household thereafter (which was fine by me, as I had no desire to ever set foot in that house again).

But, with that said, I have to acknowledge that dogs attach to their humans in a way that most other animals do not. If you treat a dog halfway decently, and meet its basic needs, it will adore you with a reverent *agape* love that we humans can only strive to emulate. Stories abound of dogs risking (and in some cases, actually sacrificing) their own lives to save their owners. Cats, um, not so much.

Like everyone else, many hospice patients have pets. The vast majority of the time, these are perfectly nice dogs or cats who get to know the hospice team members and are friendly toward us. But when their person is at the brink of death, dogs clearly sense the threat, and even the sweetest lapdog can revert to its snarling wolf ancestry. The arrival of a funeral director to remove the patient's body from the home may trigger the dog to attack the hapless man or woman who is perceived as harming the person. After hearing about an incident in which a funeral director did indeed get bitten, I made it a habit to inform all my dog-owning families that they needed to secure their dog before the funeral home staff arrived. Inevitably, the response was, "But he would never hurt a fly!" and I would have to explain to them that, under the right circumstances, Rover would not only hurt a fly, but would hurt a stocky 6'3" man.

I have not seen any cats become aggressively protective when their human dies, but there do seem to be some cats who sense approaching death. I read several stories on the internet about a cat at a nursing home in Rhode Island who would cuddle up with dying patients on the dementia unit where he lived, and a similar cat in England. At one of the nursing homes I visited, the pet cat of the dementia unit also hung out around whichever resident was actively declining.

While what follows is not a hospice story, it certainly speaks to the fact that animals are capable of understanding death and experiencing grief. In the neighborhood where I now live, there is a small lagoon surrounded by a walking path. The water attracts a variety of transient birds, but the permanent residents included a large Canada goose (named "Greyboy" by the locals) and a pair of mallards, all three of whom regularly wandered around the neighborhood. I am told that, at some point in the past, Greyboy had a mate who was hit and killed by a car. After that, he attached himself to the two ducks, and positioned himself as their protector. The three birds were always together, and Greyboy would honk loudly and begin to advance ferociously if he felt that a walker or jogger was getting too close to his beloved ducks. A short time ago (as I write this), one of the mallards was hit and killed by a car. A resident who came upon the scene shortly thereafter said that Greyboy was running around frantically. The next morning – and for the next several days when I took my morning walk – Greyboy was standing on the grass near the scene of the crime, meeping pitifully instead of his usual pugnacious squawking. It was absolutely heartbreaking.

Finer minds than my own have debated the questions of whether animals have souls, and whether they go to Heaven when they die. There are theological arguments for both sides, and I cannot compete in that arena. For the non-theologian, it is easy to believe that dogs and cats have souls and ought to be allowed in Heaven, though somewhat harder to make a case for pet mice, tarantulas, or goldfish. But the behavior of pet dogs and cats when their human is dying certainly suggests that there is a sensitivity within them that goes beyond mere biological instinct. For me personally, I very much want to believe that there is a "Rainbow Bridge" somewhere, and that someday I will be reunited with Cat, Juniper, Rosie, and the other beloved kitties that went ahead of me.

29
Waiting

As I have noted earlier, the dying process is not like you see in movies. Dying people may linger between two worlds for days or even weeks. During this time, their bodies are gradually shutting down – the kidneys produce less urine, the gut produces less stool, the heart circulates blood less effectively, and as the brain shuts down, it loses its ability to regulate autonomic nervous system functions such as heart rate, breathing, and body temperature.

But there is also some sort of spiritual work going on, which we know far less about. We get glimpses of it from the stories related by people who have had near-death experiences and then somehow come back to talk about what happened to them. Some may dismiss these experiences as merely the hallucinations of a drugged or hypoxic brain, but to those skeptics I wish to point out that none of the stories are about pink elephants or dancing unicorns, and not all of these people were on medications at the time. Others may say that these experiences are generated by the expectations of people whose religious training has taught them that they would see Heaven or Jesus or Moses at the hour of death, but I can easily refute that by the numbers of people who were *not* raised in any religion, and who espoused no faith whatsoever, until their lives were profoundly altered by their near-death encounters.

There is a phenomenon known as terminal agitation, or terminal restlessness, that is often seen in hospice patients who are approaching death. The person fights to get out of the bed, if strong enough, or flails around in the bed, if weaker. In some unfortunate cases, they may wind up injuring themselves by falling out of bed, or by banging head or limbs into the side rails of the bed, or the headboard. They may cry out repeatedly. There is usually no apparent reason for the agitation – no obvious source of physical distress. If the person is at all responsive, and you ask why they are trying to get out of bed, or what is wrong, the answer is likely to be, "I don't know...."

From a nursing standpoint, terminal restlessness is managed with medications to calm the person down. But I question whether there is some component of spiritual distress to this phenomenon. I say this because I have rarely observed it in people of strong faith, and it appears to occur more frequently in people for whom faith was not a significant element in their lives. While this is hardly tantamount to a scientific study on the matter, I base this conjecture on my observation of hundreds of hospice patients whose deaths (or near-deaths) I was present for.

When a hospice patient is, as we say, "actively dying", generally their family shows up and spends time sitting at the bedside. That is, if there *is* any family. But many of our patients who reside in nursing homes or assisted-living communities are there because they have no family, or the family does not live nearby, or they are too elderly themselves to visit with any frequency. (That, by the way, *is* the conclusion of a scientific study, which I had published in a hospice professional publication in 1994.) The staff of these facilities are too busy to sit for long periods of time simply to companion the dying resident, so I often took this task upon myself as my schedule allowed.

For me, such visits were sacred time. With no one else present to make me feel self-conscious, I could talk or sing to the person, or pray for them. From a medical standpoint, I was also monitoring the person for any signs of distress that would warrant some intervention either by the facility nurse or the hospice nurse.

When such a patient manifests terminal agitation, there are non-pharmacological interventions as well as medications. The British poet William Congreve wrote, "Music has charms to soothe a savage breast, to soften rocks, or bend a knotted oak." The hospice I worked for was blessed to have both music therapists and music thanatologists on staff.

What, you may be asking, is a music thanatologist? For a comprehensive description of what music thanatology is and does, I would refer the reader to the Chalice of Repose website: https://chaliceofrepose.org/music-thanatology. But the short answer is that music thanatology is the interface between music and medicine, a subset of palliative care in which the practitioner employs harp and voice to address symptoms such as pain, restlessness, and shortness of breath in the terminally ill. The music thanatologist does not sit down and play "Danny Boy" or "Swing Low, Sweet Chariot". He or she uses what is called prescriptive music to align with the symptom and gradually lower its acuity. No verbal description on my part can do it justice, but when I have been present for a music thanatology "vigil", it was highly effective for the patient, and extremely moving for observers, myself included.

Music thanatologists and music therapists have very different job descriptions, and in my experience, are extremely sensitive to any confusion between the two disciplines, or efforts to substitute one for the other. But each has a role in hospice, including at the bedside of the actively dying.

Mr. Whitehouse was trying to die in a grubby low-end nursing home. He had no family or friends at his bedside. He did not appear to be in any distress, but all the hospice team were surprised that he hadn't already died. As I have mentioned earlier in this book, each body has its own timetable, but this was a very frail elderly man who had not eaten or drunk anything for at least a week. If he had any unfinished business, we were unaware of it, and he was in no condition to tell us about it. As he did not have any distressing symptoms that we could see, I did not think music thanatology was needed, but I felt he deserved something more personal than simply playing his cheap radio (complete with annoying commercials) at his bedside. So I called up our talented music therapist (who played several instruments, and sang beautifully) and asked her, a tad irreverently, "Could you please come flute Mr. Whitehouse into the Kingdom?" I was not able to wait there for her arrival, but she showed up in an hour or so. She reported to me afterward that his breathing changed noticeably while she played; he died later that afternoon. Perhaps it was just his time, but it seemed to both of us that she soothed something within him that allowed him to relax and depart.

30
Give Me a Sign

Saying goodbye is rarely easy, and for many families we work with, it is truly gut-wrenching. Spiritual perspectives differ widely, and in some cases, the patient or family espouse no particular religious or spiritual belief system, or may even disdain that entire aspect of their humanness. Yet, as the old wartime adage says, there are no atheists in foxholes, and when death comes, even those who steadfastly maintain that we are nothing more than our physical bodies may find themselves wishing and hoping for some sort of indication that their loved one is somehow OK.

Mrs. Leonard was rapidly approaching death, in a GIP (hospice general inpatient) bed at one of our local hospitals, and her devoted adult children were sitting vigil around her bedside. It was December in the Midwest, and in time-honored fashion, a blizzard was wreaking havoc outside. I spent some time with the family in the morning, encouraging them to reminisce about their mother in better days, explaining some of the physical changes they were seeing, inquiring about funeral plans, and so forth – the usual things that I do at such a time. The next morning, I heard in report that Mrs. Leonard had died the previous evening, so I called the oldest daughter to offer condolences to the family, and to listen to her account of her mother's passing. She told me that, not long after I had concluded my visit with them, one of her siblings looked outside the window, and noticed a robin in the tree. Now, a robin in a tree is not inherently noteworthy, but a robin in a bare tree, in December, in a blizzard, is definitely unusual.

Mrs. Leonard had been a bird-lover, and in particular, she enjoyed robins, welcoming them as little harbingers of spring. So it was significant to the family that a robin would be perched right outside Mrs. Leonard's hospital window. Time passed, and later in the day, one of the family members again glanced out the window, and now there were *six* robins in the little tree! *One* robin sitting outside in a snowstorm is highly unusual, but *six* robins doing so, all on the same tree outside the same window, struck the children as too bizarre to be mere coincidence, and they wondered among themselves what this could mean. A short time later, Mrs. Leonard took her final breath. Amid her tears, the daughter thought to look out the window, and saw that the robins had all flown away. At that moment, she told me, she understood *precisely* the significance of the robins. The first robin represented Mr. Leonard, the devoted husband who had predeceased his wife by several years. He had come, the daughter knew, to let his beloved wife know that the time was at hand. When he came back, he brought others with him --- and at this point the daughter enumerated for me five other departed relatives who would have been a great reassurance to the mother, sort of a cosmic welcoming committee, consisting of Mrs. Leonard's parents, a couple of her siblings, and someone else – I don't recall now. Mrs. Leonard died and – as the daughter saw it – the robins had accomplished their mission, so flew away with her spirit. The family took tremendous comfort from this experience, and felt absolutely that it was a dual-purpose sign from heaven – (1) to reassure their mother as she died that she would be reunited with many loved ones who had gone on before; and (2) to reassure the surviving family that their mother was indeed going to the proverbial better place where she would be loved and cared for.

Signs from above may also come from inanimate objects. In this case, the sign was a red balloon. And this time, I was a witness to some of what happened. We had Mrs. Warshawsky as our patient only for about two weeks – not a long time, but enough for me to become seriously concerned about how her daughter was going to cope with this loss. Although Danielle was 40 years old and had children of her own, she was unmarried and had lived with her widowed mother almost all her life. Her previous attempts to separate and live an independent life had resulted in failed relationships, out-of-wedlock children, and repeated returns to the mother's apartment. In recent years, as Mrs. Warshawsky's health had deteriorated, Danielle had given up all semblance of an outside existence, and had devoted herself entirely to caring for her mother.

With death imminent, Danielle became almost zombie-like. She continued to take good care of her mother and her children, but not of herself – her hair hung in greasy strands in her face, she lost weight because she failed to eat, and her affect varied only between flat and panic-stricken. The afternoon that Mrs. Warshawsky died, I went to relieve the nurse (who still had other patients to see), and ended up spending several hours in the home. Danielle remained inconsolable, even though she was surrounded by her children and her boyfriend. It was clear that they were going to be up all night with her, and I honestly didn't feel I could do any more or better than her family was already doing, so after satisfying myself that Danielle was not actively suicidal, I left. As I exited the apartment complex that snowy evening, I noticed a large red balloon on the ground, being buffeted about by the wind. The wind in Chicago – for those of you who have never spent time there – can blow in all 4 directions at once, so I noticed with interest that the balloon was going a little bit this way, then a little bit that way, but basically staying in a relatively small area going back and forth. My interest in this was not because of any supernatural connection, however: I just wanted to keep an eye on the balloon so that I didn't inadvertently run it over, and end up with melted latex all over the underside of my car.

Normally, a family is turned over to the bereavement counselors for follow-up and support once the patient dies. I usually make a final phone call to offer condolences, but not a visit. However, because of my concern for Danielle, I decided the next week to do something I don't routinely do – make a bereavement visit. Danielle still looked quite depressed, but she was actually doing better than I had expected. In the course of our conversation she asked me, "Did I tell you about the balloon?" She then related to me the story of a balloon which had shown up on the day of her mother's death. When Danielle went outside to smoke a cigarette, she noticed a balloon hovering around in the parking lot, near the entry door. Later that evening, a wind (or perhaps a passerby) brought it inside, where it settled by their apartment door. It was at this point that Danielle and her children first said, somewhat jokingly, that the balloon was Mrs. Warshawsky's spirit, hanging around to make sure they were all OK. The next day, they got tired of seeing the balloon in the hallway, so set it free outside. But it still didn't blow away, instead continuing to hover around the immediate vicinity of the entryway. At one point, a gust of wind propelled the balloon up and over a hedge and a low fence, so that it landed on the Warshawskys' balcony! By this time, they were all taking it much more seriously that this really was some kind of sign from Mrs. Warshawsky. It did eventually disappear, though nobody in the family actually witnessed its departure. When Danielle related this story, I asked her if it was a *red* balloon; when she confirmed this, I told her that I too had seen this same balloon "hanging around" the doorway on the night of her mother's death.

This next story was my own particular sign. I don't know if anyone else in this patient's social network made this same connection or not, but it was extremely moving for me:

Joe Bridges was one of those hospice patients that I got very attached to. I try to communicate unconditional acceptance to all the patients and families I work with, but there are some people one just *connects* with, and for me, Joe was one of those guys. He was brilliant and funny, and we had quite a few quirks in common. Over the months that we had him as a hospice patient, I learned from our conversations that Joe had been in the Air Force, and had also flown a wide variety of civilian small planes and gliders. He was not afraid of danger, but was not a daredevil or a fool. He had a keenly logical and scientific mind, and had always, in his own words, "managed risk": "I never got into any situations that I couldn't walk away from," he told me. He had studied aviation and airplane design. Long after he could no longer walk, let alone fly, he still loved to talk about planes and flying with anyone who would listen. The last time I saw him – three days before his cancer death – it was apparent that the spark had gone out, and the end was fast approaching. I told him how much I had enjoyed knowing him, and how much I admired him. I said I would try to visit again later in the week, but my gut knew, as I left his house that day, that I would not see him again. Joe died on January 15, 2009. A little later that same day, a passenger jet taking off from New York's La Guardia Airport lost power to both engines just minutes after take-off. Over a densely-populated metropolitan area, in frigid weather, Captain "Sully" Sullenberger managed to guide his plane to a flawless emergency landing on the Hudson River. In what was referred to as "Miracle on the Hudson", not one of the 155 mortal souls on board was killed or even critically injured. Whatever others may believe, I like to think that, on his way up to Heaven, Joe helped one last plane to land safely.

PART VI
Miscellanea

31
It's Different When It's Your Own Family

In my introduction to this book, I shared how my paternal grandmother died, and how that experience ultimately helped lead me to this work. My other grandmother – Grammy, my mother's mother – had a very different course at the end of her life. She developed dementia, and for a long time was able to remain in her apartment with a live-in caregiver. But as her mind deteriorated, this arrangement became harder and harder to maintain. Grammy increasingly saw her caregiver as an unwelcome intruder, and when she finally forced the poor woman out the front door and into the hallway, in a torrent of accusations and expletives, she was hospitalized in a geriatric psychiatric unit pending figuring out a different plan. A few days later, I visited her there, and was glad to see that she was considerably calmer on a different medication regimen; the plan was to let her stabilize on these meds for another few days, and then return her to her home. Alas, Grammy decided the next morning to go to the bathroom without waiting for staff assistance; while walking, she began to piddle on the floor, slipped in her own urine, and broke her pelvis when she fell. So there was now no alternative but to send her somewhere where she could receive skilled rehabilitation services.

Social workers are trained not only in the classroom, but also through internships where they get practice translating their theoretical knowledge into real-life interventions. It is an excellent system, but it doesn't always work perfectly. It happened that my grandmother's discharge planning had been assigned to the social work intern on that hospital unit, and the intern only worked there 3 days a week. Since the intern wasn't there on the day that this accident happened, my mother and I were informed of the event, but not of the new timeframe for her discharge. When the intern returned the next day (a Friday), she perhaps didn't grasp the immediacy of the need to communicate with us; as a result, my mother got a call at 2PM that Grammy needed to be discharged to a skilled nursing facility by 5PM that same day!

At this point, I had been a hospice social worker for about ten years, and was very familiar with the nursing homes in my territory. I regularly assisted families who needed to place their loved one in facility. My mother lived out of state, so proximity to me was of paramount importance, as I would be Grammy's most regular visitor, and could see her in the course of my workday if she went to a facility where I had other patients. So, did my mother call *me* to help arrange placement? No, her first call was to her brother (who also lived out of state) because he had once worked as a nursing home administrator for about six months, nearly thirty years earlier! When she called me afterward, she complained to me that my uncle had been no help, and she didn't know what else to do. I gently reminded her that I do this for a living, and that I could get this accomplished with a single phone call. I asked her why she hadn't called me first, and she said, "Oh, I never thought of that...."

As I had promised, I made one phone call – to the admissions director of the best skilled nursing facility in my territory. She was someone I knew well, and liked tremendously. We had an excellent working relationship, and she was exceptionally accommodating to my plea for personal assistance. She even agreed to stay late (on a Friday evening!)

in order to meet with me and do the necessary paperwork. Grammy was delivered there via ambulance, and by 7PM all the pieces were in place.

But wait, there's more…. My mother did not want her mother to spend her final days in a nursing home. She had found a live-in caregiver, and was having an addition built to house Grammy and the caregiver; when the remodeling was complete, she would bring Grammy out to live with her. I agreed that this sounded like a wonderful plan. Since my mother, my stepfather (a retired physician), and the caregiver were all there, I did not see my grandmother for several months after this move. When I eventually flew out for a visit, I was shocked to see how much Grammy had declined: she had lost a lot of weight and looked very bony, she was no longer walking and was moved about in a wheelchair, and her speech had deteriorated to the point where it was mostly meaningless babble. I promptly asked my mother if she contacted her local hospice, and she seemed surprised by the question. Like many family members, she was too close to the situation to see the changes. I explained to her that Grammy absolutely met the hospice admission criteria for "end-stage dementia". With my mother's OK, I called the hospice, and a social worker arrived within a few hours to get the necessary paperwork signed. I was there for a few more days – enough time to make sure that the hospice team swung into action, and that their services appeared satisfactory. Grammy died three weeks after I returned home from this trip.

A prophet is without honor in her own country….

32
Dust to Dust

"All go to the same place; all come from dust, and to dust all return" (Eccles. 3:20)

From a scientific standpoint, the decomposition described in this quote from Ecclesiastes is accomplished by a variety of insects and microbes that feed on the body of the deceased, and ultimately break down all but the bones into unrecognizable tiny particles. In some unfortunate circumstances, this process can begin even before the person is dead.

Mrs. Johnson, a widow in her 80s, entered hospice as a direct admission to our inpatient unit. She was in the final stages of heart disease, and was now virtually unresponsive. What history we had – both medically and psychosocially – came from her attending physician, and a hospital discharge planner. Mrs. Johnson had been admitted to the hospital about a month earlier, due to her declining condition, and she had continued to deteriorate in the hospital despite their best efforts. Among her numerous problems, her poor heart function had led to inadequate circulation to her legs, and she had developed a non-healing wound on her right calf. When it was clear that the hospital could do no more for her, she was returned home with her right lower leg bandaged. Mrs. Johnson – who at that point was still alert and fully cognizant – was given detailed instructions on how to care for the wound so that it would not become infected. She had been living at home with her adult son – a man in his 50s – so the hospital staff felt comfortable returning her to that situation.

However, the psychosocial issues proved to be of paramount importance. The reason Mrs. Johnson's son lived with her was that he was mildly developmentally disabled. He had a part-time job retrieving shopping carts from a grocery store parking lot, and under Mrs. Johnson's patient and careful tutelage, he was able to perform the basic tasks that kept their little household running. As long as Mrs. Johnson could still pay the bills and oversee her son's activities, this was a functional symbiotic arrangement. But as her poor heart failed, she became less able to do this. Her son loved her dearly, and wanted very much to take good care of her. When she could no longer get around, he tucked her tenderly into her bed. When she could no longer provide him any guidance about food preparation (and she herself no longer had any appetite), he scrounged his own food, and lovingly brought her little cups of water or orange juice. He had no idea that she would need to be diapered, and that the diapers would need to be changed, and her bottom cleaned. He had no concept of the need to reposition her in bed. And he had no awareness of the need to tend to her leg wound.

I don't recall now exactly how Mrs. Johnson came to our hospice unit; apparently some friend or more-distant relative intervened and contacted us. I was part of the entourage that made rounds with our inpatient unit physician, Dr. G, so I was there as he examined her for the first time. She was barely able to groan a bit as he did this, so she certainly could not provide us with any information. Her poor bottom was red and excoriated from lying in her own urine. When Dr. G. uncovered her legs, he took note of the gauze bandages wrapped around her right lower leg – bandages that had clearly not been touched for days, perhaps even weeks. I'm sure the doctor and the nurse were savvy enough to be worried about what they might find when the wrapping was removed; I – at that time still a newcomer to the hospice world – did not know what I did not know, and so leaned in with great interest as Dr. G. carefully peeled off the layers of gauze. I suspect that the medical staff anticipated finding a horrible suppurating wound, so we were all shocked when we saw a neat pink *hole*, perhaps 2 inches in diameter, that went straight through Mrs. Johnson's calf! At that moment, we also saw *movement* in the hole, and Dr. G. immediately announced, "Maggots...." My scientific curiosity was immediately overtaken by revulsion, and I jumped back. Dr. G. went on to explain for the uninitiated that maggots are fly larvae; at some point, due to the son's utter obliviousness to the need for wound care, flies had been able to lay eggs in it, and in the warm summer weather they had developed rapidly. Back in the days before modern antibiotics and antiseptics, maggots were seen as a good thing, because they would eat only dead material, leaving behind the clean, healthy tissue. In Mrs. Johnson's case, the maggots had debrided her wound, keeping her from dying of sepsis. This was the only time in my healthcare career that I saw maggots firsthand.

It is one of those things that you cannot un-see.

33
Sexy Seniors

Our contemporary society would have us believe that lovemaking is reserved for the young and beautiful. Movies and TV shows portray unrealistically nubile and attractive lovers engaging in protracted bouts of wild abandon, buttons flying and zippers breaking as they tear the clothing off their partners. Closer to home, most of us have a hard time thinking about our own parents having sex. Well, they must have done it at least once because here I am, but surely they aren't *still* doing it.... *Are they...??*

Statistically speaking, the odds are pretty good that Mom and Dad are still going at it. Times have changed. Years ago, many couples believed that once the woman went through "the change of life" (a/k/a menopause), their sex lives were finished. Before reliable contraception was developed, sex was inexorably tied to pregnancy, and so many women were probably relieved to be done with the whole messy business. But as birth control became widely available, couples discovered the joys of making love purely for pleasure. And we now have those little blue pills to help older men with their erectile function (if help is needed), and an array of products to help women with impediments such as vaginal dryness and pain.

Not surprisingly, some of these sexy seniors live in retirement communities and assisted-living facilities. And if they find themselves divorced or widowed, they may start looking for love among their fellow residents. Since, for many of them, their only sexual partner for many decades was the person they married, they are often quite ignorant about sexually transmitted diseases, with the result that the incidence of STDs in such communities has been rising for many years now. (This may change as baby boomers -- who were often more sexually adventurous in their youth than previous generations – move in, but that's a research project for someone else to do.)

And yes, there are even sexy seniors in hospice. My introduction to this was Mr. Frankel. He had advanced dementia, and resided in a nursing home. His wife was a lovely woman, who had been determined to care for him at home, despite his declining cognitive status. But the sad day arrived when he no longer recognized her, and thinking her to be an intruder in the house, clocked her on the head with a heavy brass candlestick. Fortunately, she was not seriously injured, but their adult children intervened and a collective decision was made that Mr. Frankel needed to be taken care of by people who were capable of managing his paranoia and behavioral issues.

In the nursing home, Mr. Frankel began to receive some psychotropic medications that took the edge off his anxiety and aggression. But he was still a man with needs – a very, very confused man, whose executive brain functions were disappearing. And so he began trying to satisfy his needs with whichever female resident was nearby. Day after day he would be found in bed with one resident, with his hand down the pants of another, or unbuttoning the blouse of a third. This was a dementia unit, so these women were truly his victims – they had no capacity to consent, nor to fend him off. To make matters worse, Mrs. Frankel visited regularly, and often walked in on these situations, which broke her heart.

Mrs. Frankel and I had some very difficult discussions about what was going on. Keep in mind that she was of a much-older generation that didn't talk about sex, but these circumstances forced the conversation. She confided, in hushed tones, that she and her husband had not had sex with one another for many years, and in his present condition, she couldn't imagine trying to resume sexual relations with him in order to dampen his ardor for other women. I assured her that nobody would ask her to do that, but it wasn't clear what the solution would be. It was not inappropriate for him to have interest in sex, but it was not OK for him to repeatedly assault the female residents, and with his advanced dementia there was no reasoning with him. He was operating from pure unfettered animal instinct.

Needless to say, the nursing home had a huge problem on their hands, as they had a duty to protect their other residents from his predations. No amount of supervision was going to resolve this, as it would have put the staff in the position of having to physically restrain him on a regular basis. And nobody wanted to see him heavily sedated into compliance. Ultimately Mr. Frankel's attending physician prescribed (with Mrs. Frankel's consent) some form of chemical castration to reduce both his libido and his ability. This sufficed to resolve the matter until his advancing dementia and physical decrepitude made it a non-issue.

As I write these words, the issue of sexual expression in the long-term care setting is a lively topic. For the most part, these communities have become comfortable with husbands and wives sharing a room, and being allowed privacy for intimate activity. But there is no clear consensus on the more complex questions: What about gay couples? What about residents whose spouses live elsewhere, and the resident chooses to engage in sexual activities with another resident who is not their spouse? What does consent mean when one or both of the participants have dementia? What happens when a resident chooses to be intimate with another resident who is not their spouse, by mutual consent, but the adult children of one or both parties object loudly to the facility staff? I have been part of the process many times when family members and community staff were feeling their way through such situations, but the solutions were idiosyncratic to the specific circumstances, not based on broader principles regarding the right to sexual expression, or any generally-accepted definition of ability to give consent. If I were continuing in my profession longer, I would have liked to be part of moving this particular discussion forward.

34
Envy No One

Hospice nurses, nursing assistants, chaplains, and social workers do not get paid phenomenal salaries. We work very hard for our money. I used to joke that social work was the worst-paying job that anyone could do with a master's degree, but there is some truth buried in that quip. It is not my nature to be jealous of others, but when you go in and out of peoples' houses all day, every day, you inevitably notice which patients are haves and which ones are have-nots. My heart would lurch inside my chest when I had to dodge broken floorboards that were perilously patched over with a throw rug or a scrap of vinyl flooring, or when I would go to the kitchen to get my patient a glass of juice, and see that there was no food in the refrigerator. At the other end of the spectrum, I visited some extraordinarily wealthy families who had garages that were larger than my house, and walked on Oriental rugs that cost considerably more than my car. It is easy to fall into the enticing trap of believing that very rich people do not have our same troubles. As the old joke goes, money may not buy happiness, but it is still more pleasant to cry in a Mercedes than in a Chevy. However, when you actually spend time behind those imposing front doors, you learn a lot.

The elderly and pleasantly confused Mrs. Jameson had two adult daughters. The one I'll call Shannon was slim, blonde, and beautiful. She had married well, and she and her husband had a massive house in an old-money suburb. The other daughter, whom I'll call Margaret, had probably been a very attractive young woman, but now in her 50s she had grown pudgy, and the lines on her face betrayed that her life had been harder than her older sister's. She lived in a modest but neat apartment. Their arrangement was that Mrs. Jameson would live for a few months with one, and then a few months with the other, so that neither daughter was burdened indefinitely with their mother's care. She was living with Margaret when our hospice team first became involved. Shannon took me aside to whisper that Margaret had a history of substance abuse – both alcohol and pills. As far as Shannon was aware, Margaret had been sober for some time, but Shannon felt that we needed to be extra-vigilant about any medications that we put in place for their mother, to be sure that they went into the right person.

After I had been making regular visits to the apartment for several weeks, Margaret felt quite comfortable with me. In contrast to Shannon's highly controlled and proper demeanor, Margaret was a very plain-spoken person, and she told me one day that she was sure Shannon had probably warned me about her history. For reasons of confidentiality, I could neither confirm nor deny this, but Margaret went on to say that it was true: she *had* in fact abused alcohol and prescription drugs in the past. She emphasized that she was now sober, and had no intentions of allowing herself to relapse. She hinted that it was Shannon we needed to keep an eye on. However, this was moot for the moment, as Mrs. Jameson was living with Margaret.

Months passed, and it was evident that the stress of caring for Mrs. Jameson was beginning to wear on Margaret. At times she spoke sharply to her mother, and while Margaret took good care of her mother, she herself looked somewhat unkempt. The hospice nurse had not observed any medications disappearing faster than they should have, but Shannon expressed her concerns to me about whether Margaret might have started drinking again. Yet when Margaret asked Shannon to take their mother for a while, Shannon had a succession of excuses why she could not do so right away. The unhappy thought occurred to me that possibly Shannon *wanted* to see Margaret fall apart, for whatever reason. But after several weeks, Mrs. Jameson was finally moved to Shannon's house.

Shannon seemed able to meet her mother's care needs with remarkable equanimity. One reason for this was that she was able to afford a hired caregiver to come in for several hours every day, so that she (Shannon) still had time to rest, run errands, get her nails done, or go for coffee with a girlfriend. Mrs. Jameson was actively declining at this point, and was more and more confined to bed. While Shannon allowed very few glimpses behind her polished veneer, her mother enjoyed having some company, so I continued coming regularly to the house to visit with Mrs. Jameson. I got the feeling that Shannon attended adroitly to her mother's physical needs, but did not spend a lot of time just providing companionship to her. When I would come for my visits, Mrs. Jameson was always dressed in a beautiful nightgown and bed jacket, and reclining on a comfortable chair in the sunroom, but the house was enormous and Shannon occupied herself elsewhere in it.

Eventually Mrs. Jameson died in Shannon's house. Her hospice nurse was busy with another patient, so I went to the home. Shannon was as calm and collected as ever. When a hospice patient dies, one of the tasks performed by the team member who attends the death is the disposal of the patient's medications; in the pre-computer era, the name and quantity of each medication was written down on paper, and a family member would sign off on this list to confirm its completeness, and that they witnessed the hospice staffer disposing of the medications. Shannon handed me a shoebox full of pill bottles, and watched as I dissolved them all in hot soapy water and then threw the resultant slop into a plastic bag with other unappetizing garbage.

The next day, I was discussing the death with Mrs. Jameson's hospice nurse. She looked at my list of medications, and asked, "What about the Xanax?" I looked at her and asked, "*What* Xanax?" She proceeded to tell me that Mrs. Jameson had taken Xanax her whole life "for her nerves", and was on a fairly high dose while on hospice. The prescription had just been refilled a couple of days earlier, so there would have been a full bottle of it in the home. We both realized at that moment that Shannon had deliberately withheld that particular bottle from me. And it was now clear why Shannon was always so calm and collected. It was she, not Margaret, who was the active substance abuser; she had been quick to point the finger at Margaret to divert attention from herself.

I was to witness similar scenarios many times over the years. Behind the wrought-iron gates and the carved-wood front doors lurked alcoholism, mental illness, elder abuse, teenagers in legal trouble, and every other social problem you could name. Money affords a greater range of options for both pleasure and pain.

35
It's Complicated….

When is a marriage not a marriage? What does it mean to stand by your partner "in sickness and in health"? Perhaps not what you might think.

Our patient Mrs. Ellis resided in a nursing home. Even when the physical care is being provided by the staff of a nursing or assisted-living facility, someone still needs to be designated as that resident's "primary caregiver". Mrs. Ellis was on hospice for her advanced cardiac disease, but she also had moderate dementia, meaning that major decisions about her care had to be directed to her primary caregiver. "It's her *ex*-husband," the young facility social worker said to me with a slightly-raised eyebrow. She offered no further explanation of the situation. My immediate assumption was that the couple had divorced at some point, but that Mr. Ellis was probably a basically decent fellow who had stepped up to the plate when his ex-wife took ill and really needed someone to look out for her.

For my initial assessment visit, I asked Mr. Ellis when he would next be at the nursing home, and said I would like to meet with him then. He was quite amenable. We met up at Mrs. Ellis' room, and I was surprised when they greeted one another very affectionately, with hugs and kisses. I doubt that Mrs. Ellis understood that she was enrolled in a hospice program, but she seemed content with my explanation that I was a social worker who wanted to meet the two of them. We had some inconsequential chatter for a little while, until one of the staff came to whisk Mrs. Ellis to the dining room for lunch.

Once Mr. Ellis and I were alone, I had to ask. "I understand that you and Mrs. Ellis are divorced…," I began. "Yes, but let me explain," he interrupted. He proceeded to introduce me to the concept of a "Medicaid divorce", which at that point I had never heard of. First of all, he hastened to tell me, he loved Mrs. Ellis dearly. But although they were financially comfortable, they were not rich. Mr. Ellis was a practical man, and when he had to bring his wife to a nursing home for care, he realized that she might live long enough for those expenses to exhaust all their savings. Accordingly, he brought her to a nursing home where she could go on Medicaid when the money ran out. The spousal impoverishment rules would allow him to keep about $100,000 in assets (besides their home), but they had several times that amount in their joint accounts, and there was no telling how much longer either of them might live. Their attorney had pragmatically advised Mr. Ellis to get a divorce; if they split their joint assets 50/50, he would get to keep about $300K instead of $100K, and her half could still be used to meet her expenses. Legally, once her $300K was gone, she would be eligible for Medicaid, and if she died before that happened, he was still the beneficiary of whatever was left.

Mr. Ellis devotedly spent time with Mrs. Ellis nearly every day, and she died never knowing that she was a divorcee. She never did go on Medicaid.

Sarah was a 71-year-old woman with early-onset dementia. Her husband Mark told me that she had first manifested symptoms nearly ten years earlier. Dementia comes in many varieties, and this was certainly not a classic Alzheimer's-type, but her ailment had never been definitely diagnosed – it was somewhat moot, since there was (and still is) no cure for any type. Throughout most of her decline, she had continued to live at home with her husband, but in the past year, her needs had become overwhelming (and he was getting older), so he had placed her at an assisted-living community that specialized in dementia care.

Sarah was pathetic – there was no other word for it. The framed photos in her room showed that she had once been a vibrant and beautiful woman, but there was no trace of that woman now. Her formerly neatly-coiffed hair now hung limply about her face. She had lost – and was continuing to lose – weight, so her attractive clothes sagged and bagged. Every few months, Mark would bring in several new outfits in a smaller size, and within weeks, those too were hanging off her tiny frame. Even in this condition, she looked much younger than her chronological age, which made the situation even sadder.

But the most pathetic thing about Sarah was that she had become zombie-like. When she was awake, she wandered incessantly. Although she did not seem to have a vision deficit, she had lost the ability to *comprehend* what she saw. (The fancy name for this is visual agnosia.) She would walk into a wall and then just stand facing it until someone would come to rescue her, because she could not understand that it was a physical barrier that she could circumvent by walking in another direction. She would try to pick up a pattern off a tabletop, or she would pick up some item of décor (such as a vase) and carry it around with her, and then randomly let go of it when she got tired of holding it. She no longer recognized her husband, and indeed he could scarcely engage her attention most of the time when he would visit. Occasionally, if she was tired, he could get her to sit down next to him and slump against his shoulder; then he would put an arm around her, and for a few minutes at least, they would cuddle and he could imagine that this was all just a bad dream.

Over time, Mark became comfortable enough with me to confide his inner struggles. He loved Sarah deeply, and had no intention of abandoning her. At the same time, he was a man with a need for companionship and affection, and Sarah was incapable of providing either. He said that he felt disloyal even thinking about other women, but Sarah's illness had already dragged on for nearly a decade, and he did not want to live out his days alone. I did what a social worker is supposed to do in this situation: I listened and provided emotional support, without telling him what he should or shouldn't do.

When you go in and out of nursing homes and assisted-living facilities day in and day out, you inevitably establish relationships with members of their staffs. Some of those are purely business, but sometimes, real friendships emerge. One of the people I became friendly with at this particular community was Leona, one of the administrative staff. She was divorced, and hoping to someday meet the right guy. She worked at this assisted-living facility for about a year, and then one day disappeared. The scuttlebutt was that she had been fired, though none of the staff volunteered any reason why she might have been. I did not have Leona's personal phone number, so I couldn't call her to ask. But – because the long-term care world is like a chessboard, with perpetually-moving pieces in a small area – I assumed she would track me down through my employer when she landed in her next job.

Time marched on. Sarah continued her slow decline. One Saturday night, my husband and I went out to a local restaurant for dinner. We were engrossed in our own conversation when I heard someone call out, "Debbie!" I turned in the direction of the voice, and saw Leona sitting several tables away. She and her date each had a glass of wine in front of them, and she looked radiant. It took a moment for it to register with me that her dinner companion was Mark. When it sank in, I reached out and put a hand on each of their shoulders. "I am so, *so* glad to see both of you happy," I told them.

No doubt, there will be some who read these stories and feel that Mark and Mr. Ellis were terrible faithless husbands. But while neither of them adhered to the letter of the law about marriage, I feel that they both embodied the spirit of it. Both gentlemen did what they needed to do to take care of themselves, but were thoroughly present to take care of their wives also.

36
Occasionally I Saved a Life

It doesn't happen often, but occasionally I have had the opportunity to save someone's life. Mr. Maxwell was one such person.

The history was this: Mr. Maxwell was a 57-year-old gentleman with a history of several chronic illnesses -- multiple sclerosis (though he was not seriously impaired by it at this point), hypertension (not well controlled), and diabetes. Several days earlier, he had had a stroke at home – no doubt related to his poorly-controlled high blood pressure -- and his frantic wife had him taken to the ER. Although the stroke did not initially seem that severe, its effects extended over the next day or so, and he became completely unresponsive. Many tests were done, and the doctors concluded that Mr. Maxwell was unlikely to recover to any significant degree.

When his wife was informed of this assessment, she did a complete about-face. Whereas up to this point she had been very anxious for medical science to go all-out for her husband, she now swung into action as the staunch defender of his right to die in peace. He had executed a living will many years ago – which she brandished about -- stating that he never wanted to be kept alive as a "vegetable". She insisted that the tube-feeding – which had been initiated as an interim emergency measure – be discontinued, and wanted all testing and telemetry stopped. This greatly rattled some of the nurses in the intensive care unit, who felt that Mrs. Maxwell was now trying to *kill* her husband to avoid being saddled with the care of an invalid. The doctor made a referral to our hospice, but the nurses made sure our staff was aware of their suspicions. As the hospice social worker, I was asked to visit ASAP to determine what was really going on.

I met with Mrs. Maxwell, and did not at all feel that she was trying to end her husband's life for selfish reasons. Perhaps she was a supremely-savvy psychopath, but I don't think so. She was well-aware what some of the ICU nurses were thinking about her, and she was understandably angry about it. She talked at length about their life together, his various illnesses, and so on. Like most people, she was not enthusiastic about the possibility that her husband might live for a long time in a vegetative condition, but it seemed to me that she was looking at this very much from *his* perspective – namely, that *he* would not want to live that way. It is easy for those who have not been in a comparable situation to pass hasty judgment on a decision-maker who seems a little too eager for the patient to die. Our society does not provide a lot of good options in these circumstances. The societal expectation is that a good wife will do everything in her power to take care of her invalid husband at home, or if that is not possible, will at least pay for a private-duty caregiver or a nursing home for him. But not everybody can afford to do this. Mrs. Maxwell was now the sole support of her household. They had only one child – a young adult daughter who lived and worked in another state. So Mrs. Maxwell and I also discussed the practical ramifications of his care. She was aware that he could go to a nursing home under Medicaid if he survived, so that she did not need to quit her job to take care of him, or bankrupt herself to pay for his care. However, again, she was very clear that *he* would not want to go on living in such a diminished state of existence, no matter how his care was rendered. Just because we have the technology to preserve biological existence, doesn't necessarily mean that it is the *right* thing to do. Mrs. Maxwell, in my assessment, was not trying to kill her husband – she was simply arguing for his right to die a natural death from his stroke, without extraordinary measures being imposed upon him. I felt that this was a valid perspective, and told her she had the hospice team's support for her decisions.

When a hospice patient is being cared for in an inpatient setting, we are required to evaluate that patient on a daily basis to determine whether he or she continues to meet the criteria for inpatient eligibility, because Medicare and other payors pay more money for inpatient care than for care provided in an outpatient setting. This means that a hospice nurse sees the patient every day. To meet this requirement seven days a week, our hospice would send an on-call nurse on Saturday and Sunday. Our assumption with Mr. Maxwell was that – in the absence of any artificial feeding – he would simply remain unresponsive, and quietly decline towards death. Mr. Maxwell happened to be admitted to hospice on a Thursday, so the hospice nurse who regularly went to this hospital saw him again on Friday, at which time he was still unresponsive, but slightly agitated. Over the weekend, the on-call nurse – who had not seen Mr. Maxwell before – visited, and reported to the team on Saturday that she had found him to be somewhat responsive. Her Sunday report was that he was significantly more responsive, made eye contact with her, and was able to answer yes/no questions appropriately with a nod or shake of his head, though he could not speak.

This news changed everything. Not only was he getting better rather than worse, but he was recovering his ability to communicate. Mrs. Maxwell, as her husband's power of attorney for healthcare, was his decision-maker only because he had been unresponsive from his stroke. It was now imperative to discern quickly whether he had regained enough

cognitive capacity to make decisions for himself. At the start of
the workday on Monday, I was on the phone with his regular
hospice nurse to discuss our course of action, and an hour later,
we were standing at Mr. Maxwell's bedside.

"Good morning, Mr. Maxwell," I greeted him. He opened
his eyes and looked right at me. "My name is Debbie, and I'm
a hospice social worker." I had no idea whether or not he knew
what "hospice" meant, but candor was the order of the day
here. With the hospice nurse as my witness, I asked the patient,
"Do you know where you are?" He looked around the room,
somewhat quizzically, and shook his head no. At this point, I
told him the Reader's Digest version of his situation: he was in
the hospital, after a severe stroke. He had been completely
unresponsive for most of a week. He had had surgery, and had
a big incision on the left side of his head. It appeared that his
swallowing and his speaking ability had been affected by the
stroke. I asked if he understood what I was saying, and he
nodded. I asked him to wiggle the fingers of his left hand, and
he did so. I then asked him to wiggle the fingers of the right
hand, and they did not move. So I told him that it appeared that
the right side of his body was also impaired by the stroke. I
gave him a moment to digest all this new information, then
proceeded carefully. "Mr. Maxwell, I know that you have a
living will. When you were unresponsive, your wife explained
to us that you would not want to be kept alive if you were only
going to be a 'vegetable', so she did not want you to have a
tube feeding." I tried to word this cautiously, because I didn't
want to make it sound like she had seized the first opportunity
to do him in. He nodded his understanding, and I proceeded.
"Now that you are waking up, the situation is very different.
Your prospects for improvement are better, and it looks like
you are able to make decisions for yourself again, so I need to
know how you feel and what you are thinking – OK?" He

nodded. Although he could not speak, I could see in his eyes that I had his rapt attention, and that he was comprehending the subject matter. "Mr. Maxwell, are you hungry?" He nodded, and I locked eyes with the hospice nurse. "Mr. Maxwell, we will need to talk to your doctor and see what he thinks, but would you be interested in going to a skilled rehab facility to try and see how much function you can regain?" Again, a nod. The nurse then explained to him that she would contact his doctor to communicate this change in condition, and to obtain the necessary orders for tube-feeding, a swallow evaluation, and a possible transfer to a skilled nursing setting. Based on what our patient was telling us, it seemed appropriate that he be discharged from hospice, because he wanted to try his best to live and recover at this point.

Now all that remained was the hard part: informing his wife, who was completely unaware of the momentous turnaround that had just taken place. I phoned her at her nearby office. Of course, when she saw the hospital's phone number on her caller ID, she immediately assumed that the worst had happened. So I explained that indeed there had been a change in condition, but in the opposite direction from what we all had expected: her husband was alert, oriented, and able to communicate! After she had recovered from her shock at this development, I went on to tell her that – from a legal standpoint -- this meant he was now able to resume making decisions for himself. The nurse and I had talked with him for some time, I informed her, and he had indicated that he understood his medical condition, that he was hungry and wanted to be fed, and that he wanted to try skilled rehab and work towards recovery. Mrs. Maxwell said she would be right over. When she arrived, we talked somewhat further about all of this, and she was very grateful that her husband had somehow been granted this second chance at life. We wished them both the best of luck, and I said that this was my very favorite way to lose a hospice patient.

I would like to be able to say that he made a full recovery and they lived happily ever after, but life is not that neat and simple. For one thing, hospice and skilled rehabilitation (for the same diagnosis) are mutually exclusive, so in order to pursue rehab for the effects of his stroke, he had to revoke from hospice. This meant that we had no further right to access his medical information, and therefore we never learned what happened after that fateful day. For another thing, nobody is guaranteed a full recovery. Only time would tell what abilities Mr. Maxwell might regain, and whether he ultimately could achieve a level of functionality that would make him feel that his life was worth living. His wife had welcomed his turnaround as a second chance at life, but would they both look at it that way a year down the road if he were still wheelchair-bound, unable to speak, and dependent on tube-feedings? What is a challenge to one person may be an insurmountable obstacle to another. And I wondered about Mrs. Maxwell's conscience, and the possible impact of her decisions on their relationship. Might she at some future point – with 20/20 hindsight – feel guilty about deciding so quickly to stop all interventions and call in hospice, even though she was advocating for his wishes, based on the medical consensus at that time? Might he at some point be angry with her for seemingly giving up on him? I hope not, and every time I think about this situation, I feel great sympathy for them both, but especially for her.

I had another opportunity to try to save a life many years later. Mr. Firestone was dying from the final stages of some sort of cancer. He and his wife were both in their mid-70s and had been married for many years. They were extremely sweet people, clearly devoted to one another. Their two adult daughters loved their parents, but lived a considerable distance away, had fulltime jobs, and were raising their own children, so were unable to be as helpful as one might have wished. Mr. Firestone was a very undemanding person, and was quite content to rest in bed most the time, so in theory Mrs. Firestone could have taken time to get her hair done, go for lunch with a girlfriend, or some other self-care activity, but she didn't. Other than necessary excursions to the nearby grocery store, she never left the house, and somehow managed 99% of his care needs herself (the remaining 1% being handled by the hospice team members who visited throughout the week). She was absolutely old-school, seeing his care as her wifely duty, and accomplishing this without even the slightest whiff of martyrdom. On my weekly visits, I often brought coffee and pastries for them, determined to get Mrs. Firestone to enjoy some little something that was pleasurable. She appreciated the gesture, and over the course of the months of her husband's illness, she came to confide in me about many things.

One day Mrs. Firestone mentioned to me that she had a urinary tract infection and had called her doctor. Apparently he knew her well, and was willing to write a prescription for antibiotics without first having her come into his office. When I visited the next week, Mrs. Firestone updated me that the prescription did not appear to have helped, and she was going to ask him for a different medication. I asked her what symptoms she was experiencing, and she said that she had had some bleeding in her underwear. A couple of weeks passed in which we did not discuss this again. Then one day, she happened to phone me in between our usual scheduled visits. I don't recall what the original reason for her call was, but in the course of conversation, she mentioned that she was still having this bleeding, despite having been on two different antibiotics. I felt an alarm go off in my brain, and I asked her if she was sure that the bleeding was indeed coming from her urethra. Her response shocked me, because it made me realize that she was extremely naïve about her own anatomy: despite having birthed two children, and despite presumably decades of menstruation, she had clearly never looked at or touched her own vagina. I was grateful that we were on the phone, because my face undoubtedly would have betrayed my disbelief. I took a deep breath and tried to keep my tone calm as I told her that it was extremely important that she find out which orifice the blood was coming from. She had no idea how to do this, so I painstakingly talked her through the process of using a hand mirror to locate her vagina, and then gently inserting a clean washcloth with one finger just an inch or so into the opening. She called me back after she had done this, and informed me that I was correct: the bleeding was coming from her vagina. I instructed her to call her doctor *immediately* and tell him this. Of course he now insisted on seeing her right away, and within a fairly short period of time, she was diagnosed with uterine cancer.

At the start of this story, I said that I had the opportunity to *try to* save a life. I would like to report that this story had a happy ending, but ultimately it did not. Mrs. Firestone's doctor wanted to do a hysterectomy as soon as possible, and follow it up with cancer treatments. However, Mrs. Firestone had to weigh the pros and cons in her own mind. If she had the hysterectomy, she would be quite incapacitated for a while from the surgery itself, and would be under lifting and driving restrictions for many weeks. Their daughters could not take over Mr. Firestone's care for that length of time, and it was not financially possible for her to hire a live-in caregiver during that period. She was adamantly unwilling to consider placing her husband temporarily in a skilled nursing facility while she recuperated, especially since she would be unable to drive to visit him. So she concluded that any surgery or treatment for her own cancer would have to wait until after her husband had died. It was not what I wanted to hear, but I could understand it from the perspective of her value system. It was another couple of months till Mr. Firestone died, and Mrs. Firestone continued to devote herself entirely to him. Of course, once he had died, I had no legitimate reason to keep in touch with her, so I could only hope that she had taken appropriate steps to address her own cancer once he was gone.

A couple of years passed, and I had no reason to expect that I would ever learn the outcome. Then one day, on the list of patients who had been newly admitted to our hospice inpatient unit (IPU), I saw the name "Firestone". Sadly, it was the same Mrs. Firestone, now dying from her cancer. Although she was not assigned to me, I hastened to the IPU, eager to see this lovely woman one more time. I read in her chart that she had had the hysterectomy, but too late: the cancer had already spread to other parts of her body. Her nurse noted that one of the daughters had visited briefly, the other not at all thus far. I would not have recognized the frail little form in the bed if I had not known her name. She was skeletally thin and bald, with sunken eyes and cheeks, barely breathing. She was minimally responsive, and when I spoke to her, I could not see any spark of recognition. That was the last time I saw her. On one hand, it broke my heart that she had met such a fate, and that I had been unable to prevent it. On the other hand, I had to acknowledge that her choice was the ultimate act of self-sacrificing love.

37
Roadrunners

Over the years, I have observed certain patterns of behavior that characterize certain patients. One such pattern has to do with the progression of the terminal illness. Non-medical people generally assume that all terminal diseases follow a straight downhill trajectory that looks rather like a descent down a mountainside. That mountainside may be steep, or more gradual, but it is linear and downhill all the same. While that does happen at times, in my experience the course of most terminal illnesses is more like a rollercoaster ride, and indeed many family members use the term "rollercoaster" to describe both the ups and downs of the illness, and the ups and downs of their attendant emotions. There are periods of relative stability, punctuated by crises, and gradual recoveries from the crises, but never quite to the level that was baseline previously. The overall trajectory is still down, but not at all in a linear way. Patients and families are often baffled by these inconsistencies, and I hear comments like, "The doctors in the hospital said that Mom is terminal, but now she seems to be getting *better!*" Until the next crisis....

But there is also a third pattern that I see frequently. It is neither the straight downhill nor the rollercoaster. I call these patients "roadrunners". To explain that name, let me remind you about (or acquaint you younger folks with) the old "Roadrunner" cartoons of my childhood. "Wile E. Coyote" was forever trying (in vain) to catch the "Roadrunner", who always outsmarted him. In some of the episodes, the roadrunner would trick the coyote into running off the end of a cliff. Thanks to the wonders of cartooning, the coyote would run well past the end of the cliff, pause to look down and realize there was no ground beneath his feet, then drop like a rock. (Technically I should probably call these patients "coyotes", but that word has come to have a very different meaning nowadays.)

Some patients do the same thing. These tend to be people who have always been very strong and/or independent. If she is female, she may have been a caregiver to many – more comfortable giving care than receiving it. If he is male, he may be former military – someone who has been trained never to show weakness of any kind. At the end of their lives, these patients cling tenaciously to their self-sufficiency, long past the point where other people would have given in to dependence. If he can no longer cook a meal, he subsists on microwaved frozen foods. If she cannot climb the stairs on her feet, she will resolutely bump up and down them on her bottom. She will conceal her severe cancer pain from even her closest relatives. Then one day, there is some crisis, and a day or two later, he is dead. Family members are shocked, because he seemed to be doing so well. But in reality, he ran past the end of the cliff, and then dropped....

Beth Shapiro was a roadrunner. The referral to hospice came from the social worker (I'll call her Kathy) at a suburban township office, and it was her last-ditch attempt to provide some sort of help. From a medical standpoint, Ms. Shapiro was a 73-year-old childless single woman with ovarian cancer. But her medical problems were the least of the issues. And the story that I was to become a part of highlighted the challenges of trying to help someone who does not want the help being offered.

I spoke to the township social worker before making my initial visit. She explained that Ms. Shapiro used to come to the local senior center periodically, but had a rather abrasive personality, and the regulars disliked her. Because of her visits there for free coffee and the occasional meal, however, Kathy had become very familiar with her, and actually rather fond. Eventually Ms. Shapiro began to show up less frequently at the senior center, and finally stopped coming altogether; Kathy didn't know why at the time. Unbeknownst to Kathy, Ms. Shapiro's belly had begun growing rapidly, and she ultimately had to stop driving because she could not comfortably fit behind the steering wheel. But Ms. Shapiro carried on with her life. One winter day, she slipped and fell on her icy driveway. She was not injured, but because of her enlarged abdomen, she was unable to get back up. A passing motorist saw her struggling, and called 911. The paramedics were able to get her up, and she said she only wanted them to help her walk safely back to the doorway of her house. But that is not their job description: an elderly woman had fallen on concrete, and they felt strongly that she needed to go to the ER, to make sure she had not broken a bone or gotten a concussion. Finally she agreed to be assessed in the ER, but she first needed to fetch her purse and coat. That proved to be her big mistake, because when the paramedics glimpsed the inside of her home, they were so appalled that they called the township office to report the conditions.

At the hospital, it was determined that Ms. Shapiro had not done herself any damage in her fall, but the ER physician was understandably concerned about her enormous stomach, especially after learning that Ms. Shapiro had no idea what was causing it but had just assumed that it was cancer. One thing led to another, and Ms. Shapiro was admitted to the hospital for a work-up that she was unenthusiastic about, as she did not want any treatment. Meanwhile, wheels had been set in motion at the township office: an inspector was sent to her home while she was hospitalized, and found it in a deplorable state. Long-neglected plumbing issues had resulted in a sodden, rotting bathroom floor. Ms. Shapiro's indoor-outdoor cats had long since ceased to use their litter box, and there were lumps of cat feces all over the carpeting. A hole in the roof left the house vulnerable to water damage and rodent invasion. The house was promptly declared uninhabitable, and the hospital discharge planner was informed. However, as abrasive and feisty as Ms. Shapiro might be, she was neither incompetent nor stupid. She flatly refused to go to any skilled nursing facility, and insisted on returning to her own home. And she played her sympathy card adroitly: she told Kathy that she had just been diagnosed with terminal cancer, she was not going to have any surgery or treatment, and just wanted to be allowed to return to her home to die. It was at this point that Kathy relented, and called us.

My initial assessment visit was interesting indeed. It was clear that Ms. Shapiro was a woman of strong opinions and clear priorities, most of which were a few standard deviations from the norm. She was quite paranoid, but she was also very bright and very sarcastically funny – I found myself liking her immediately. She seemed comfortable with me, or at least as comfortable with me as she was with anyone, and I was quickly invited to call her Beth. I was to learn (belatedly) that she liked people in direct proportion to their usefulness to her; since I brought her treats, and didn't challenge her too much, she liked me. She reeled in the rest of the hospice team easily, and soon we were all doing little extras for Beth that we didn't necessarily do for our other patients. She was remarkably pain-free, and did not want to take any medications that might impair her ability to function alone in her house. The bedside commode offered by the hospice nurse was refused because Beth could not clean it herself, and had nobody else to do this for her; she determinedly waddled to her rotted bathroom right up to the end. A couple of neighbors took pity on her and brought her homemade soup and other ready-to-eat foods. She shared just enough of her background with me to reveal that she had been terribly abused as a child, had never married, and had no children. She had relied on herself all her life thus far, and planned to keep on doing so as much as possible. She was not a well-to-do woman, but her retirement income was sufficient for her basic needs. She stopped paying all but the essential bills; instead she used some of her money to pay for new bedroom windows, so that she could be warmer (despite the hole in the roof) and could better watch the world going by from her bed.

As the weather began to get warmer, Beth started wanting to go out, and we had to lay down the law that we were absolutely not allowed to take her for a ride anywhere ever. Beth was savvy enough to know that she qualified for a state-subsidized caregiver a few hours a week, and I made the application for her. The hospice team hoped that this companion could provide some much-needed housekeeping – we were tired of dodging piles of cat poop on our visits – and hands-on care, but Beth only wanted someone who had a car. Since she was the employer, she won out: the caregiver was only too happy to drive Beth to local fast food restaurants (where Beth would pay for both of their lunches) or to the local dollar store, and not have to do any unpleasant work.

Another, more unfortunate, consequence of the warmer weather was that Beth's quasi-feral cats ushered an invasion of fleas into the house. We were all starting to get severely bitten during our visits. Beth got extremely defensive when this was brought to her attention, staunchly denying that there could possibly be fleas in her home. No amount of evidence persuaded her, and it was getting harder and harder for the team to be in the house. I visited to extend to her the hospice's extremely-generous offer to arrange and pay for a fumigation; Beth responded by angrily cussing me out and firing us. I called Kathy, the township social worker, to inform her of this unhappy development. Beth was noticeably declining by this point, so neither Kathy nor the hospice team felt good about what had happened.

Eventually, I learned the rest of the story. The state-subsidized caregiver continued her visits: since she either took Beth for a drive, or sat with her on the front porch, she didn't have to deal with the flea infestation. One day, less than two weeks after our hospice had been fired, the caregiver arrived and found Beth dead in her bed. As far as anyone knows, Beth never had a day during her final illness where she allowed herself to become fully dependent on the care of others. Beth was the consummate roadrunner.

38
The View from the Other Side of the Nametag

As a hospice professional, I grew very accustomed to wearing my nametag, and bringing comfort to hospice patients and their families. As a hospice professional, I stood at hundreds – perhaps even thousands – of bedsides, educating families about the dying process, and offering words of sympathy when their loved ones died. And as a hospice professional, it was easy to lapse into the belief that death happens to everyone else's family, but not my own.

One spring day in 2017, I sat with my sister-in-law Ruth as she signed paperwork, and a kind nurse admitted my 96-year-old father-in-law, Al, to the hospice program that I worked for. Less than twenty-four hours later, while I was sitting in my team's weekly meeting, I received a call from Ruth that Al had just died. The hospice professional persona was briskly ripped away as I teared up, made hasty apologies to my teammates, and ran out of the office. Word spread quickly, and on my long drive to the suburban nursing home where Al resided, I began getting texts from coworkers who had just heard the news. I felt so much comfort knowing that the social worker (aptly named Grace) who had been assigned to Al was already on site, supporting my family members.

When I got to Al's room, Grace spoke the same simple words of condolence to me that I had said to others so many times. A few moments later, the team chaplain appeared, and offered similar consolation. I welcomed them, because in this moment of grief I felt completely de-skilled – one of the family, not one of the hospice staff. Although we had been preparing ourselves for weeks for Al's probable death, we were still caught off-guard by its suddenness. Like so many hospice families, we thought we had a little more time; after all, his nurse-practitioner had told us only yesterday that she thought his prognosis was about two weeks. Even though we family members were supporting one another well, I was surprised by how comforting it was to have the hospice social worker and chaplain there with us.

In the summer of 2020, I went to visit my mother and my 93-year-old stepfather in Florida. I had not seen them in several months, and was concerned by how much frailer my stepfather Victor appeared. I told my mother before I headed back home, "I feel like I'm seeing him for the last time." The next couple of weeks were indeed the beginning of his precipitous decline, with increasing confusion and weakness, and multiple trips to the hospital. One day, after my mother had had to call 911 for him three times that day, I told her, "It's time to call your local hospice." I did the recon, made the phone call, and he was quickly admitted. One of my stepbrothers flew in and encamped at his father's bedside for the next several weeks, while I did my best to provide moral and logistical support by phone. Each time the hospice nurse visited him, my mother called me so that I could hear the nursing assessment and be part of the conversation. Even though my mother had private-duty caregivers and my stepbrother on hand to help with Victor's physical care, the various hospice team members were a godsend, providing medical guidance, supplies and equipment, and their congenial presence. The day that I was packing my suitcase and readying my car for my return to Florida to help out, I received the call that Victor had just died. I drove back to Florida as quickly as I could to support my family.

In the days after my father-in-law's death, and again after my stepfather's death, I was deeply touched by the presence (either literally or in cyber-space) of friends, relatives, and hospice staff. People who had, in some cases, never met them checked in via phone calls, e-mails, sympathy cards, or Facebook to say those simple little words, "I'm so sorry for your loss." To be frank, I was surprised to discover how much those little gestures meant to me. When you have worked in hospice for a long time, it can sometimes seem almost rote to say those six words to families. I sometimes questioned whether it even made a difference. The answer to that question, I realized now, lay not in the weightiness of our interactions, but in the mere *fact* of them. Showing up, being present, acknowledging our family's loss, *matters.*

And that is how it looks to me, from the other side of the nametag.

Post-Mortem

When I took my first job in the field of hospice, I was quite naïve about the real nature of the work. I pictured myself sitting on the edges of my patients' beds, holding their hands as they took their final breaths. I envisioned having deep conversations with them in which I helped them make peace with their illness and impending demise. I expected that their families would rally around them, provide loving care, and bathe them in lavender water while singing hymns when they died. I was the hero of my daydreams, bringing all this to fruition with my phenomenal skills and wisdom. With the aid of my tender ministrations, everybody would have a picture-perfect comfortable death, and all their families would be uplifted by the experience.

The reality of the work initially slapped me in the face. I had no idea how to deal with abject poverty that made even basic care unachievable. I was not prepared for substandard nursing homes that reeked of urine, while demented residents howled in their wheelchairs or fell out of their beds. I could not have anticipated the depth and breadth of family dysfunctions that resulted in physical, emotional, and financial abuse of the patient. I did not know that my caseload would include schizophrenics, old Nazis, racists, and the occasional small child. In my first year or so on the job, I had quite a few moments where I questioned whether I was cut out for hospice, or indeed, even for the practice of social work. It did not help that I was also going through a very traumatic divorce from my children's father early in my career, which knocked me off-center for a considerable period of time.

Then, two things happened that began to make it better. One was that a social worker from another local hospice reached out to the various hospice programs in our area, and suggested that we social workers start a monthly supervision group wherein we could share our experiences and our practice wisdom with one another. This group continued for several years, and we all learned and grew tremendously as we supported one another.

The other thing that happened was that I began to get myself centered again. After my divorce, I recognized that I had two beautiful little boys to raise, and that I needed to reconnect with my own spiritual strength in order to not just survive but actually thrive as a single working mother. The details of how this came about could be the topic of an entirely different book, but I began attending a Bible study group and recreating a faith-based support network for myself. In addition to helping me revitalize my relationship with God, this group was also where I met Stuart, the man who eventually became my husband. He has been the wind beneath my wings for over a quarter-century now.

It began to become very clear to me that, while I thought I had chosen a career, I had actually stumbled onto my calling. As I worried less and prayed more, the spiritual nature of the work became the foreground, and all those other concerns, the background. I began to look at each patient encounter as a divine appointment, and to allow myself to be used as God's hands, feet, and voice. Although hospices in the U.S. are generally secular organizations, I started to discover that many of my coworkers also personally operated from a basis of their own faith, whatever it might be. I became bolder in my approach to my patients and their situations, and felt empowered to seek new opportunities – doing professional and community presentations, writing articles for professional journals, and eventually stepping into a new role as a hospice team manager (which I did for seven years). In all of these endeavors, I maintained a perspective that I was working for the Lord first, and for my employer second.

Nobody who works in hospice for many years can remain unchanged by the experience. I have heard this sentiment voiced innumerable times by nurses, chaplains, social workers, and other frontline hospice staff. But I have also heard it from hospice administrative assistants and other office-based workers who have never seen a patient firsthand; many of them tell how they have been deeply affected by the stories they hear from the patient care staff.

I too have been mightily changed by thirty years of hospice work – perhaps I should call it hospice ministry. I am stronger, because my patients' struggles have put my own struggles into proper perspective. I am quicker to speak out, and to take action, because I no longer take tomorrow for granted. And I have seen that, when everything else falls away, the most important things in life are our connections with other humans who love us, and with our Creator.

Someone asked me recently if I left hospice work because I felt "burned out". The simple answer to that is no. But, in my early 60s, it began to feel very difficult to keep up the physical pace that the job demanded, especially with fiscal pressures forcing my employer (and many other hospice programs) to require higher caseloads and larger geographical territories for their frontline staff. I prayed long and hard about what to do, not wanting to abandon my ministry. I began to get the sense that God was reassuring me that thirty years was sufficient. In confirmation of this, my husband and I found ourselves with an opportunity to do some traveling that we had previously thought would have to wait until we reached full retirement age. We both left our fulltime jobs, put our house on the market, and took a big leap of faith. If there is one solid lesson to take from hospice work, it is don't wait until retirement to do the things that you've always wanted to do, because you never know what may happen tomorrow. We loaded our camping gear into our truck, and traveled the U.S. and Canada for five months, before deciding to relocate to Houston, Texas, where two of our adult children were already living.

I know that I am a better person for having done this work. I can only hope and pray that I have given as much to my patients and their families as they have given to me.

Here are a few things that I have learned, and that I now share with you:

1. If there is something that you have always wanted to do, go do it. Find a way to make it happen, and don't wait until you retire. Tomorrow is not guaranteed to any of us.

2. Keep a healthy perspective on your problems. If you are not actively dying today, be thankful. You have another day in which to try to make things better.

3. If your life sucks right now, reach out to someone else who has even bigger problems, and try to help them. It is amazing how, in helping another human, we so often receive more than we give.

4. If you do not already have a faith tradition, find something that you can believe in, and place it at the center of your life. I am not proselytizing for any particular religious belief here. The important thing is to acknowledge that *something* – be it a deity or a set of principles – is bigger and more powerful than your individual self.

5. Most importantly, never take the good things for granted. The universe doesn't owe us a darn thing. If you have a spouse, partner, friend, parent, child, or pet

who loves you dearly, love them back, and appreciate them. If you can walk, see, taste, hear, feel, breathe, and think, rejoice in those things. If you have $50 in the bank, food in your refrigerator, and a couple of changes of clothes, you are more fortunate than many people in the world. Always, *always*, be grateful.

I am exceptionally grateful to have been so blessed by my hospice career.

Acknowledgments

Over the course of a thirty-year career as a hospice social worker, I have been privileged to work with many phenomenal people. I deeply regret that I cannot possibly name or thank them all individually here, but I want to mention a few who contributed most significantly to my evolution as a hospice social worker and as a human:

Nancy Flowers, my supervisor for my first field placement during my MSW program. With infinite patience, she showed me how to translate classroom knowledge into practice wisdom, and when we ceased to be student and teacher, we became friends.

Dr. Martha Twaddle, who was the brilliant medical director of Hospice of the North Shore when I first started working there, and who remained a coworker in various capacities for decades thereafter. She was and is a fine specimen of human being, the walking embodiment of the integration of body, mind, and spirit. Whenever I talk about one of my linguistic pet peeves – the confusion of the words "imminent" and "eminent" – I say, "Dying patients are *imminent*. Dr. Twaddle is *eminent*."

Sharon McCarthy, who was the "wise elder stateswoman" of the social work department when I came to Hospice of the North Shore. She saw something in me that I did not see in myself, when she recommended me to higher-ups as a potential clinical manager of a hospice team. Sharon is still who I want to be when I grow up.

Julie Bruno, who was the head of the social work department at Hospice of the North Shore when I started working there. Passionate about doing the right thing, and doing it well, she educated me in ways too numerous to mention. As a supervisor, she was unfailingly fair, calm, and even-handed, even though (as she said) managing social workers was "like herding cats".

Larry Reed, Jennie Anderson-Nowak, and **Shari Russeau** – hospice team managers who had the wisdom not to micro-manage me, and who allowed me to be myself and find my own way. All of them were secure enough in their leadership skills to recognize my concerns and questions as reflective of my genuine desire to learn and contribute, not "pushback". I always felt respected by them, and in turn, gave them my best.

Sandy Cashman, who was my regional director for the final years of my stint as a hospice clinical manager. A lively mix of intellectual brilliance, deep compassion, and a sense of humor, she not only mentored me as a leader, but also advocated for my team and for me. She is a wise woman, and a good friend to this day.

Dr. Jordan Grumet, a colleague and an accomplished author in his own right, who took time from his own busy schedule to encourage me to write.

Last, but far from least, the many hospice patients and their families that I have worked with during these 30 years. You don't know it, but you gave me far more than I gave to you. Thank you for the education, and the memories. I am honored to have been able to serve you.